AIR FORCE RECORDS
A Guide for Family Historians

PART I

CHRONOLOGY

1878 - 1918

1862   Investigation and experiments begun by Lieutenant George Edward Grover R.E. on the subject of military aeronautics. In spite of the lack of support he received from official sources, he, more than any other officer, deserves the title of the "Father of English Military Aeronautics".

1878   Experiments with balloons at Woolwich Arsenal under Captain James Lethbridge Brooke Templer, 2nd Middlesex Militia, and the Balloon Equipment Store established under Captain R.P. Lee, R.E.

1882   Balloon Equipment Store moved to the School of Military Engineering, Chatham.

1883   Balloon Establishment consisting of a small balloon factory, depot and school of instruction establishment at St. Mary's Barracks, Chatham. A ball-court was roofed over and turned into an erecting shop.

1883   The first balloon was made at Chatham by Captain Templer with the assistance of Captain J. E. Capper, R.E. This was the Sapper of 5,600 cubic feet. The envelope was made of silk soaked in linseed oil, which was squeezed out after impregnation by a household mangle. Hydrogen was made in old beer barrels with spetter and sulphuric acid, and cleaned by passing through water. Another balloon, the Heron, of 10,000 cubic feet capacity with an envelope of gold beater's skin was also made and was so successful that gold beater's skin was standardised for envelopes.

1884   Three sizes of balloons were standardised: 10,000 (T. Class), 7,000 (S. Class) and 5,000 (F. Class) cubic feet capacity. Several balloons were made in these three sizes. A successful method was evolved for storing hydrogen in steel cylinders at 2,100 p.s.i.

1886   Balloon school established at Lidsing, near Chatham.

1887   Major J.L.B. Templer officially apointed "Instructor in Ballooning" by War Office. First Air Estimate of £600 per annum.

1889, June   Balloon detachment sent to Aldershot to take part in summer manoeuvres, followed by a recommendation that the Balloon Establishment be moved from Chatham to Aldershot. Major Templer re-appointed "Officer in Charge of Balloons" in addition to "Instructor".

1890   Balloon Section, Royal Engineers, formed. Depot moved to Aldershot, and erection of buildings commenced at South Farnborough, near the canal. Air Estimate voted £4,300.

AIR FORCE RECORDS
A Guide for Family Historians

William Spencer

the national archives

First published in 2008 by
The National Archives
Kew, Richmond
Surrey TW9 4DU
United Kingdom

www.nationalarchives.gov.uk

The National Archives brings together the Public
Record Office, Historical Manuscripts Commission,
Office of Public Sector Information and Her Majesty's
Stationery Office.

© Text copyright William Spencer 2008

A catalogue card for this book is available from
the British Library.

ISBN 978 1 905615 25 4

Jacket, typographic design and typesetting by
Ken Wilson | point 918

Printed in Great Britain by
The Cromwell Press Ltd., Trowbridge, Wiltshire

COVER IMAGES: (centre) aircrew about to board an Armstrong
Whitworth Whitley bomber, the RAF's first 'heavy' bomber,
which took part in the first raid on Berlin, August 1940. (Photograph by Getty Images/Davis); (above) a Bristol F.2B, a
fighter used by the Royal Flying Corps in the First World War.
(Photograph Q 011980 courtesy of the Imperial War Museum)
FRONTISPIECE: Chronology of RAF establishment,
Farnborough. AIR 1/686/21/13/2245
PICTURE CREDITS: The photograph of the balloon in South
Africa (COPY 1/444) was registered to Horace W. Nicholls,
40 Friar Street, Reading, Berks in January 1900 and appears
courtesy of the Royal Photographic Society, Bath. The photograph taken from the Royal Aero Club Certificate of A.B.
Spencer (Fig. 17) appears courtesy of the Royal Aero Club and
the Royal Air Force Museum. The Memorial Plaque of A.G.
Fox (Fig. 13) appears courtesy of Dave Morris. The photographs of A.B. Spencer as a Petty Officer, RNAS (Fig. 15) and
of the RAF Long Service and Good Conduct Medal (Fig. 36)
appear courtesy of the author.
IMAGES IN THE TEXT: Figs 4 (Q 68460), 7 (HU 89340), 12 (Q
12063), 21 (Q 012051) and 45 (CH 8945) appear courtesy of
the Imperial War Museum, London. The rest of the images in
this book are taken from the files of the National Archives and,
unless otherwise mentioned, are © Crown copyright.

ACKNOWLEDGEMENTS

I should like to thank the following people for the
help, information and guidance they have given
me: Hugh Alexander for his assistance with
regard to illustrations; the archival staff at the
Fleet Air Arm Museum; Jan Keoghane and Jerry
Shore for help with Arthur Bedward Spencer;
Peter Elliot and the archival staff at the RAF
Museum for help with Royal Aero Club Certificates and their own archival holdings; Dave Morris for the loan of various items relating to Alan
Geoffrey Fox; and Paul Baillie for his extensive
insight into the surviving RAF honours and
awards files. My colleague Lee Oliver must be
thanked for producing the list of abbreviations.

I would also like to thank the other two thirds
of the editorial team: Catherine Bradley and
Janet Sacks.

My final thanks must as always go to Kate,
Lucy and Alice for allowing me to neglect my
duties in order to update this guide.

WILLIAM SPENCER

CONTENTS

USING THE NATIONAL ARCHIVES

The National Archives is the best place to search for an ancestor in the armed forces. Most of the records described in this guide can be consulted at The National Archives, Ruskin Avenue, Kew, Richmond, Surrey, TW9 4DU. The archives are open 09:00–17:00 on Monday and Friday, 09:00–19:00 on Tuesday and Thursday, 10:00–17:00 on Wednesday and 09:30–17:00 on Saturday. The National Archives is closed on Sundays, public holidays, and for annual stocktaking. The National Archives website address is:

www.nationalarchives.gov.uk

The National Archives is about ten minutes' walk from Kew Gardens Underground Station, which is on London Transport's District Line, as well as the London Overground Service. For motorists it is just off the South Circular Road (A205). There is adequate parking.

The National Archives can be a confusing place to use. If you are new to researching there, it is a good idea to allow plenty of time to find your feet. The staff are both knowledgeable and friendly, and are happy to help if you get lost. There is a public restaurant and a well-stocked bookshop on site. Self-service lockers are available to store your belongings.

Accessing the records is simple. First you need to obtain a reader's ticket, which is free, when you arrive. Please bring two forms of identity, such as a passport or driving licence and a credit card or bankcard, to validate your address and signature. If you are not a British citizen you will need your passport. For further information see:

www.nationalarchives.gov.uk/visit/whattobring.htm

It is possible to get photocopies and/or digital copies of most documents you find: please ask the staff for details. It is possible for you to use your own digital camera to copy documents.

In order to protect the documents, each one of which is unique, security in the reading rooms is tight. You are only permitted to take a notebook and notes into the reading rooms and can only use a pencil. Eating and drinking are not permitted in the reading rooms.

The records held by the National Archives are described and ordered using a three-part reference. The first element is known as the 'department' and takes the form of letters. The 'department' denotes which government department created the records. The second element is known as the 'series' and collects together records of a similar type. The second element is in the form of numbers. The third and final element of a document reference is known as the 'piece' and this usually is just a number but occasionally may include letters.

Over time, terminology used to describe the document references at the National Archives has changed and you may hear terms such as 'letter codes' and 'class' still being used. 'Letter codes' are of course the 'department' and 'class' is the 'series'. Whilst such terminology is interchangeable, many of the 'department' identities, irrespective of whether they are being called 'department' or 'letter code', are obvious, with WO being the War Office, ADM being the Admiralty and AIR being the Air Ministry. Other 'department' identities are not so obvious; the records of MI5, for example, are identified by the letters KV (it's an anagram of significance for you to work out) and the Welsh Office uses BD. Most squadron operational record books for the Second World War are, for example, in the series AIR 27. It is these department and series references that are referred to throughout this guide.

Brief descriptions of every document (piece is the term used by TNA) are in the series lists. Several sets of lists are available in the Open Reading Room and other locations. The series list gives you the exact reference of the document you want. This is what you order on the computer terminal. Occasionally in this guide we use the full reference, written thus: AIR 27/724.

An increasing number of documents are available on microfilm, microfiche or in digitized format. Where this is the case, the fact is noted in the text. You do not need to order microfilms on the computer as you can help yourself to them in the Open Reading Room.

In addition, there are various other finding aids for genealogists. The best general overview is provided by Amanda Bevan's revised *Tracing Your Ancestors in The National Archives* (7th Edition, TNA, 2006).

The structure and development of the War Office is fully described in Michael Roper's handbook *The Records of the War Office and related departments, 1660–1964*.

The National Archives Online

As well as giving information on where the National Archives is, opening times and how to gain access, the National Archives website gives details about popular records, including research guides and lists of independent researchers. Most importantly, the website allows readers to access the National Archives Catalogue (series lists).

The Catalogue can be searched by using keywords, dates and, if you know them, the department (letter code) and series (class) where records are known to exist.

Follow these simple steps to identify the documents you require:

1 Locate the Catalogue.
2 Click on *Search the Catalogue*.
3 Type keyword(s) into the top box, the year (as appropriate) into the two boxes below the keyword box and, if known, the departmental code and series (optional) into the last (bottom) box.
4 It is possible to use more than one keyword, either by just putting the words in or by doing a combined word search linking the words together with AND.
5 Click on *Search*.

The computer will then search for documents of interest that include the search term(s) you used and that are included in a document description. Document descriptions and the references under which they will need to be ordered will be listed as either individual items or, in the case of multiple results, under the department code (the letters) and then with the number of results in blue at the right-hand side. Click on the blue number to obtain more detailed descriptions of these results.

Many records have been and are being digitized and placed on the DocumentsOnline section of the National Archives website. Amongst these records are the First World War Army Medal Index Cards (WO 372), the Women's Royal Air Force records of service (AIR 80) and the Second World War Royal Air Force Combat reports from AIR 50. In each case it is possible to search these records by name and, where appropriate, to download them for a fee.

ROYAL AIR FORCE.

Form 3677 Z. (MEMBER).

WOMEN'S ROYAL AIR FORCE.

CERTIFICATE OF DISCHARGE
ON DEMOBILIZATION

(MEMBER).

(1).

No. _18549_

Name _Adams M._

Rank _Member_ _Mobile._

Air Force Trade _Waitress_

Enrolled on _30 – 9 – 18_ at _Sheffield ._

Demobilized on _____ at _– do –_

(2). DESCRIPTION.

Age _20 years_

Height _5' 6"_

Build _Medium_

Eyes _Blue_

Hair _Fair_

(3).

Her work during the time she has been in the Force has

been _Satisfactory._ _H.O.i/c Demob._

No 2 Aircraft Repair Depot. R. A. F.

Signature of Commanding Officer
carrying out Dispersal.

Her personal character has been _Very good,_

S. Russell. ae

Date _10.10.19_

Signature of W.R.A.F. Officer

(519) Wt.42056/G643 1/19 80M (6) D.St. (12)

INTRODUCTION

Aviation has always been a great interest of mine. From when I had a flight in an Auster on my seventh birthday, through 13 years as an aircraft engineer in the Fleet Air Arm, to being Principal Military Specialist at the National Archives, aircraft and the people who designed, built, flew and maintained them have always fascinated me and continue to be part of my working life.

As military aviation is a relatively new part of military history, the associated records held by the National Archives are also new, especially in relation to the age of the greater part of the archive. The study of military history, especially the First World War and Second World War, is extremely popular, not just with genealogists but also with those who have an interest in the different aspects of warfare and military service. This guide stems from a similar interest, but primarily from a desire to see all of the salient information put into one place.

This year sees the 90th anniversary of the creation of the Royal Air Force. Researching the flying services continues to be as popular as ever. The careers of famous pilots, and indeed many aircrew, have always been closely scrutinized. Less well known but just as important are the careers of the personnel of the flying services who remained firmly on the ground, and also those RAF personnel who served at sea.

Now that records of service relating to individuals in the Royal Flying Corps (RFC), Royal Naval Air Service (RNAS), the Royal Air Force (RAF) and Women's Royal Air Force (WRAF) have been released up to given dates, information can be gleaned about many of these personnel, who form a very important yet neglected part of aviation history. Together with the operational records of the Royal Engineers Balloon Section, Royal Flying Corps, Royal Naval Air Service, Royal Air Force, Fleet Air Arm, Glider Pilot Regiment and Army Air Corps—many of which have been available for a number of years—it is now possible to study complete aspects of aviation, from high command down to individual pilots and ground crews.

This guide consolidates and updates information about all of the records relating to individuals of the flying services in one place. It also

Fig. 1 *Typical WRAF record of service* (left), *which can now be searched for by name and downloaded from DocumentsOnline.* AIR 80/2

provides information about records which were either not available or were not covered in depth when *RAF Records in the PRO* was published, and reveals the way in which certain records have now been made available since the publication of *Air Force Records for Family Historians* in 2000 (both titles are long out of print). From the pioneering Royal Engineer balloonists of 1878 to the operational records of the RAF, the Fleet Air Arm (FAA) and the Army Air Corps (AAC) in the post-1945 period, this guide brings together the key records created by the various government departments involved in the administration of the flying services and their personnel.

Using the National Archives and accessing the records held there is now far easier than even five years ago. With the advent of the online Catalogue, it is possible not only to identify records before you arrive at the National Archives, but also to carry out keyword searches of the Catalogue, thereby letting the computer do the work of turning pages to find the records required. See the 'Using the National Archives' section in this guide for more information about the online Catalogue.

Contrary to popular belief, archives never stand still. New records are still being accessed, while other records that have been available for some time are now delivered in different ways, such as by computer in the form of digitized images of the original paper. Although there are numerous operational records available up to the early 1980s, the records of service of men and women who saw service after the early 1920s are still held by the Ministry of Defence (MOD). Records of service were once held for 75 years by the MOD for administrative purposes, but more recent legislation has meant that they may only be made available 100 years after the birth of the subject individual. Consequently, when the records of service that are currently less than 100 years old are released, the study of aviation and the men and women who were part of it will continue.

The format of this guide first places each of the flying services into its historical context. It then concentrates on providing guidance about the records where information on individuals may be found. New ways to identify and access archives via electronic catalogues, digital formats and the internet are making such information ever more accessible. Much more research can now be carried out remotely, rather than having to visit the building where the archives are held. As a result the records—and the remarkable stories they contain—can be enjoyed by an increasingly wide audience. I hope this guide will enable researchers to use their time more productively, and to find the answers that only original records can provide.

WILLIAM SPENCER

1 MILITARY FLYING UP TO 1914

As with anything new in the armed forces, innovative ideas and technologies tend to be regarded with trepidation, fear and even contempt. It is only through trial and error that we learn how to use the new to best effect, and how to integrate it into an established environment. So aviation had to find a way of fitting into the Army and Royal Navy, and the two services had to learn how aviation could be used to best advantage for their purposes. To adopt, adapt and integrate aviation in the armed forces took time, especially as each service went about it in a different way to satisfy their own needs.

1.1 The Royal Engineers and their Balloons

Although the use of balloons was discussed by the War Office at least as early as 1804 (WO 30/71), effective use of them only started in 1878, when a number of experiments were conducted at Woolwich Arsenal. These experiments were accompanied by the creation of a Balloon Equipment Store, and by 1879 the Royal Engineers (RE) were using a few officers and men to conduct further trials.

After balloons took part in Army manoeuvres in 1880 and 1882, a balloon detachment accompanied the Bechuanaland expedition in 1884 and another detachment went to eastern Sudan, taking part in operations around Suakin (see 8.1 for operational records).

The Balloon Section Royal Engineers was authorized in May 1890. The Balloon Equipment Store, which had been at Chatham since 1883, was now separated from the Balloon Factory and School, which moved to Farnborough. The Balloon Equipment Store remained at Chatham as the depot, but in 1892 moved, along with the Balloon Factory, to Aldershot, where it became the School of Ballooning.

During the Boer War, Nos.1, 2 and 3 sections, RE Balloon Section served in South Africa, whilst No.4 section saw service in China (see 8.1 for operational records).

After the Wright Flyer (the first powered aeroplane) had flown in 1903,

been put on board from Woolwich Arsenal at the
ecemeal state, altogether unsuited to Service con-
were now designed and manufactured in Cape
with suitable fittings, and an arrangement for
will in any position of the balloon. The some-
e arrangement devised at Chatham for continuous
th the aid of a battery, vibrating sounder, and
l, abandoned. A very much simpler and more
ubstituted, consisting of a pair of the improved
These give a much louder and more audible
ich pattern. They are fitted with a simple and
the necessity for batteries, vibrating sounders,
with.

in the gear were also remedied. The screens
wind were set up in different situations to prac-
Flag signalling was gone on with when time

Ballooning Operations at Mafeking, 6th to 18th April, 1885.

On April 6th ballooning operations proper were undertaken. Work commenced at 6 a.m. by raising the poles and screens to shelter the balloon during
inflation. Two hours before breakfast were spent in glycerining the upper half
of the "Heron," 10,000 cubic feet. This process would of course have been
dispensed with had there been any sudden or pressing demand for the balloon
on service. The object of it was to render the gold-beaters' skin envelope more
soft and supple, as in going through the Tropics and the great heat experienced
at Cape Town, and on the journey up country, it had become somewhat too
dry and harsh.

Owing to this dryness, and consequent tendency to crack, a hole was torn
in the balloon early this day. It was, however, quickly repaired by the Sappers,
who are trained to the work.

We devised and practised for the first time this day a simple and easily
applied process for rendering the envelope soft and supple. Its value was
confirmed by subsequent experience on the following days.

I do not propose here to go into the details of it. It may be regarded as
a satisfactory solution of the difficulty created by the drying up of the envelopes
in very hot and dry climates, which I have always hitherto looked upon as
formidable.

Towards midday the weather turned out very squally and unfavourable.
As, therefore, no order had been given by the General Officer Commanding for
an ascent, the filling was stopped and the balloon bagged down about $\frac{4}{5}$ths full.

7th April.   Next morning work was commenced at 6 a.m. We found two or three
small holes in the envelope which were causing leakage due doubtless to the
too great dryness of the envelope yesterday morning before the balloon was
damped down. These were quickly and easily repaired. The weather was
somewhat windy and unfavourable early, but calmed down towards midday.
Major Elsdale reported progress to the Commanding Royal Engineer and
General Officer Commanding, and received instructions for an ascent. The
filling of the balloon was accordingly resumed. The General Officer Commanding came and inspected the balloon, the arrangements for inflating and securing
her, and the whole of the gear about 3 p.m. The remaining gas necessary to
complete the inflation was now turned in, and the balloon prepared for an
ascent. She was conveyed away from the protection of the screens to a convenient locality adjoining, and Major Elsdale made a good ascent to a height
of about 500 feet. This represents an elevation of considerably over 5,000 feet
above sea level, from which all ballooning altitudes should be reckoned. The
"Heron" was then hauled down and the General Officer Commanding got into
the car, and made a good ascent remaining up about 10 minutes. The weather
was very favourable for observing, and he obtained a most excellent view.

Next several Officers of the Staff made good ascents. The General Officer
Commanding then went up again. He was conveyed, while still at a good

a developing interest in aeroplanes began to influence the Balloon Section, to such a degree that changes were inevitable. After experiments with both airships and aeroplanes between 1908 and 1911, the Air Battalion of the Royal Engineers was authorized in February 1911, with the new battalion becoming effective from 1 April of the same year.

As the new Air Battalion grew, and aircraft of all types illustrated their military potential, so the size and status of the Air Battalion was investigated by the Committee of Imperial Defence. Britain had in fact been left behind by several of European countries that had already created separate air services. A Technical Sub-Committee of the Committee of Imperial Defence eventually concluded that a separate air service was needed, and the product of these conclusions was the creation of the Royal Flying Corps on 13 May 1912.

1.2   The Royal Flying Corps

The establishment of the Royal Flying Corps (RFC) on 13 May 1912 finally acknowledged the importance of military aviation (CAB 38/20). Numerous records concerning the RFC and its expansion and development can be found in AIR 1, from the recruitment and training of RFC personnel to the design, manufacture and purchase of aircraft and the establishment of units and their preparation for war.

1.3   The Royal Naval Air Service

The Royal Naval Air Service (RNAS) did not really exist as a separate service by name until July 1914. Before then the RNAS was the Naval Wing of the Royal Flying Corps, staffed by officers and men who had volunteered from other branches of the service.

Naval interest in aviation dates back to 1908, when Captain R.H.S. Bacon, Director of Naval Ordnance, put forward a proposal for the construction of a rigid airship to be used for fleet reconnaissance.

There are numerous sources, both primary and secondary, which can provide details relating to naval aviation. By far the most useful secondary source is *Documents relating to the Naval Air Service 1908–1918* by Captain S.W. Roskill. This is full of National Archives document references, and a copy is available in the Library.

A file listing the number of officers and men in the RFC Naval Wing at Farnborough in July 1913 can be found in AIR 1/763/204/4/196.

Fig. 2 (left top) *Royal Engineers Balloon Section in South Africa 1899–1902.* COPY 1/444

Fig. 3 (left) *War Office report on RE Balloon Section operations in South Africa in 1885.* WO 33/44

2 ROYAL FLYING CORPS, ROYAL NAVAL AIR SERVICE AND ROYAL AIR FORCE UP TO 1918

Times of war provide an opportunity for risk taking and trial and error unheard of during peacetime. Not only did the RFC and RNAS expand greatly between 1914 and 1918, but the service chiefs also realized how important aviation was – so much so that they created a new service.

2.1 The Royal Flying Corps

With the outbreak of the First World War, the RFC was at last given the opportunity to show what it could do and how aircraft could contribute on the battlefield.

The structure of the RFC altered as the size of the British Expeditionary Force changed. As early as November 1914, the RFC was formed into two wings of two squadrons each: No.1 Wing served the First Army and No.2 Wing the Second Army. As the Third, Fourth and Fifth Armies were created so the RFC adapted itself accordingly. In August 1915 each Army became supported by an RFC brigade made up of two aeroplane wings and a balloon wing. This structure remained until the end of the war.

The Order of Battle for the RFC and RAF from 1914–18, showing which squadrons were with which superior units, can be found in AIR 1/2129/207/83/1.

2.2 The Royal Naval Air Service

Although there was a naval wing of the RFC prior to 1914, it was not until July of that year that the Royal Naval Air Service (RNAS) became a separate entity. Personnel strength of the RNAS between August 1914 and March 1918 can be found in AIR 1/626/17/60.

Rough notes on the early development of the RNAS covering the period 1912–17 can be found in AIR 1/625/17/1, and a short history of the service can be found in AIR 1/682/21/13/2226.

Fig. 4 (above) *Lieutenant-General Sir David Henderson, considered by many, including Trenchard, to be the true father of the RAF.*

Fig. 5 (right) *RFC Orders for March 1914 showing duties, postings and promotion of RFC personnel.*
AIR 1/805/204/4/1158

ORDERS   No 58.

by

Lieut.Colonel F.H.Sykes, Commanding Royal Flying Corps.
=*=*=*=*=*=*=*=*=*

Monday. 9th March 1914.

Part I.

Orderly Officer for tomorrow.	Lieut Hon J.D.Boyle.
Next for duty.	" H.F.Glanville.
Orderly Sergeant for tomorrow.	Sergeant G.Laing.
Next for duty.	" H.Page.
Sergeant of Guard for tomorrow.	" T.Hughes.
Next for duty.	" G.Laing.

2. Attachments.

No 266 Sergeant J.Aspinall, No 2 Squadron, is attached to No 6 Squadron from the 6th instant.

3. Leave of Absence.

Lieut E.F.Chinnery is granted leave of absence from 13:3:14 to 12:4:14, with permission to travel in Turkey and Greece.

4. Examination (c).

The undernamed qualified for promotion to the rank of Major and Captain respectively, in subject (c), King's Regulations, Appendix XI, at the examination held at Aldershot on the 2nd and 3rd March 1914:-
    Captain (tempy Major) A.D.Carden.
    Lieutenant G.I.Carmichael.
    "   G.B.Hynes.
    "   J.N.Fletcher.
    "   L.C.Hordern.

5. Claims - Settlement of.

The following instructions from the Command Paymaster, Aldershot Command, are published for information:-
"In view of para 337 A Financial Instructions please note that all claims for the current financial year should where possible, reach this office duly completed not later than the 24th inst.
Regarding lodging claims, they should be prepared and passed to the Officer i/c Barracks for signature in time to admit of their receipt in this office by the date quoted above".

6. Detail for tomorrow, 10th instant.

4 men to report to Officer i/c Stores at 8.30 a.m.

Part II.

1. Postings.

The undernamed are posted as stated:-

No 1136	2nd A.M.	H.G.Henderson.	5:3:14.	Recruit.
,, 1137	"	C.J.A.Thomas.	3:3:14.	"
,, 1138	"	E.Hart.	27:2:14.	"
,, 353	Sergeant	R.Baughan.	6:3:14.	From No 2 Squadron
,, 73	1st A.M.	A.Ward.	"	to No 6 Squadron.
,, 276	"	M.Weare.	"	do.
,, 106	"	G.Langfield.	"	do.
,, 283	"	J.Hart.	"	do.

2.3 The Royal Air Force and Women's Royal Air Force

The Royal Air Force (RAF) and Women's Royal Air Force (WRAF) were formed on 1 April 1918. Manpower for the RAF came from the Royal Flying Corps and Royal Naval Air Service. Many of the women were new entrants, but some did come from the Women's Army Auxiliary Corps.

The basic operational structure of the RAF was the same as that of the pre-April 1918 RFC. However, the biggest operational change to take place after the formation of the RAF was the creation of the Independent Air Force, whose task was to carry out strategic bombing of targets in Germany.

Historical notes about the WRAF can be found in AIR 1/681/21/13/2212.

The development and operations of the RFC, RNAS and RAF during the First World War are covered in *War in the Air* by Sir W. Raleigh and H.E. Jones, a copy of which can be found in the Library.

3 ROYAL AIR FORCE, FLEET AIR ARM, GLIDER PILOT REGIMENT AND ARMY AIR CORPS FROM 1919

Once the RAF became a permanent force, so its structure and organization changed and evolved. As peacetime moved towards war, so the RAF adapted itself to meet the oncoming threat. Today the RAF continues to adapt and change according to its needs.

After the creation of the RAF in April 1918, the Admiralty basically lost control of its air assets, such as aircraft on HM ships, to the RAF. In 1924 the Fleet Air Arm of the RAF was created from seagoing air assets. Between 1918 and 1937 most seagoing aircraft were flown and maintained by RAF personnel.

In July 1937 the Fleet Air Arm was passed back into Admiralty control under the guidance of the Air Branch of the Royal Navy.

In the Second World War, military aviation was further developed due to service and operational requirements. The need to create new units to operate and support aircraft in these new roles led to the formation of the Glider Pilot Regiment and the Army Air Corps.

The following information places the flying services into their historical contexts and provides a guide to understanding the terminology used at specific times.

3.1 The Royal Air Force

The manpower of the RAF started to be reduced soon after the First World War, and especially after the signing of the Treaty of Versailles in 1919. Once Germany had been defeated, an air force of such size was seen as unnecessary. By January 1920, the RAF had demobilized over 250,000 men. However, at the same time, new tasks for the RAF were being considered. By far the most important task the RAF was to undertake between 1919 and 1939 was that of colonial policing. The best book on this subject is *Air Power and Colonial Control* by David Omissi.

As the RAF was virtually a wartime creation, the manpower within it were nearly all wartime volunteers only. In 1919 plans for a permanent RAF were drawn up and in subsequent years many of the administrative

<u>25th Jan 1920.</u> Eil Dur Elan (cont'd)

along coast about 5·0 miles east of Las
Khorai. To land at Las Khorai fill
up & continue bombing if targets
presented themselves.
The coast was carefully searched
but no signs of reported Dervishes
or stock seen.
Machine landed Las Khorai 15.40.
Three machines left Las Khorai 16.35.

      5548   Gray + Green.
      669   Russell & Liftley
      679   Hobson & Roberts

Orders To ~~bomb~~ locate & bomb Enemy
& stock reported 25 miles East of
Burnt 1º.
A careful search was made as
far as Burnt 1º. Nothing seen with
the exception of five or six flocks
of sheep 12' west of Las Khorai,
these belonged to Friendlies. Machines
returned to Las Khorai at 17.55.
5548 had to land 2½ miles away
from Las Khorai on account of water
in Petrol.
N.B. From the results of aerial recco
the report that large quantities
of stock were proceeding West
along the coast appears to be
incorrect

structures and institutions as we know them today were created.

Between 1919 and 1939 many changes took place with regard to how the RAF operated its aircraft. From the First World War period squadrons, wings and brigades became squadrons, groups and commands. The United Kingdom was split into two commands, known as area commands, which were split into inland and coastal areas, each with numbered groups representing different parts of the country. These two commands were the two key operational parts of the Air Defence of Great Britain (ADGB).

Two further commands in the United Kingdom at this time were Cranwell and Halton Commands, responsible for the training of officers and airmen respectively.

Outside the United Kingdom, overseas commands in various parts of the Empire continued the colonial policing role that prior to 1914 had been solely undertaken by the Army. India, Iraq, Palestine, Middle East and Mediterranean were all overseas commands between 1919 and 1939.

The biggest changes to RAF structures to occur before the outbreak of the Second World War were the abandonment of the Air Defence of Great Britain Command and the formation of separate commands relative to the task each aircraft type was allocated. In place of the ADGB came Fighter Command and Bomber Command. Newly created commands included Coastal Command and others responsible, for instance, for balloons, training, co-operation with the Army and maintenance. Operational Record Books (ORBs) and other command papers for these organizations can be found amongst the AIR record series.

ADGB was re-formed during 1943 when the major part of Fighter Command was dedicated to defending Great Britain. The other part of Fighter Command was used in the creation of the 2nd Tactical Air Force. The designation ADGB was abandoned again in 1944, with Fighter Command returning to its previous name.

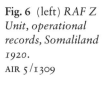

Fig. 6 (left) *RAF Z Unit, operational records, Somaliland 1920.* AIR 5/1309

Fig. 7 (below) *Bristol Fighter aircraft of 31 Squadron RAF in the inter-war period, an aircraft type used many times in minor operations in the 1920s.*

Changes to manpower requirements between the wars saw the creation of the Auxiliary Air Force (AAF) in October 1925 and the Royal Air Force Volunteer Reserve just prior to the outbreak of the Second World War. AAF squadrons saw considerable success during the Second World War, when they were given numbers in the 500 and 600 range. Further details can be found in *RAF Squadrons* by C.G. Jefford.

The creation of an RAF nursing service (later the Princess Mary's Royal Air Force Nursing Service) occurred in 1918. Details concerning its establishment can be found in AIR 2/93.

Operational records of the inter-war years can be found in 8.5.

The advent of the Second World War saw the RAF adapt to the operational and strategic needs of the conflict. Various changes took place, including the creation of special units, such as 617 Squadron, and whole air forces, such as the 2nd Tactical Air Force (2 TAF). For operational records of the Second World War period see 8.6.

Beyond the changes to command structure and the creation of various squadrons during the Second World War, the single most important creation of this period was the RAF Regiment described below.

3.1.1 *The RAF Regiment*

The Royal Air Force Regiment was originally formed as the RAF Aerodrome Defence Corps in 1942. Created to protect airfields, the RAF Regiment has served in numerous operational theatres around the world. Records concerning the regiment can be found in AIR 2, Series B, Code 90, with specific files AIR 2/4880 and AIR 2/5378 concerning its formation and early history. Further files concerning manpower, its formation and role, and another history are in AIR 20/2027, 3658 and 4032, respectively. Operational records of the RAF Regiment are discussed in chapter 8.

Further exploits of the RAF Regiment and its forebears can be found in the book *In Adversity – Exploits of Gallantry and Awards to the RAF Regiment and its Associated Forces 1921–1995* by Squadron Leader N.G. Tucker, RAF.

3.1.2 *The RAF since 1945*

As occurred after the end of the First World War, the RAF has undergone a number of administrative and structural changes since 1945. As the British Empire has gradually shrunk, so the global character of British military commitment has changed. From being the main deliverer of Britain's nuclear deterrent until the 1960s, the roles and responsibilities of the RAF have likewise continued to change.

For those carrying out research into the activities of the RAF since 1945, only the operational records and records relating to awards are so far in the public domain. Changes to RAF commands since 1945 are not the responsibility of this guide. The current RAF structure can be found at *www.raf.mod.uk*.

3.2 The Fleet Air Arm

After the First World War the RAF took control of all aspects of aviation, although the Royal Navy was responsible for the aircraft-carrying ships. Although the Fleet Air Arm (FAA) was created officially in name in 1924, administrative control of naval aviation and naval aircraft was the responsibility of the RAF and was only returned to the Royal Navy in 1937. The complexities of this inter-service rivalry are best explored by reading Stephen Roskill's *Naval Policy between the Wars*. The restoration of Admiralty control of naval aviation was a result of the Inskip Report, a copy of which can be found in AIR 8/223.

The majority of FAA squadrons are numbered between 700 and 899, those in the 700 range being second line units and those in the 800 range, front line. A number of other numerical ranges have also been used. For a brief history of all the FAA squadrons, see *Squadrons of the Fleet Air Arm* by Ray Sturtivant.

As has similarly happened to the Army and RAF after 1945, the FAA has diminished in size but not effectiveness, and has been involved in numerous operations around the world.

A history of the RNAS and FAA covering the period 1903–45 can be found in AIR 20/6349. Further histories of the FAA can be found in ADM 335.

3.3 The Glider Pilot Regiment and Army Air Corps

Created as the direct result of an instruction from Winston Churchill in June 1940, the Glider Pilot Regiment (GPR) and its administering corps, the Army Air Corps, (AAC), were established in February 1942. The Army Air Corps was also responsible for the Parachute Regiment and Special Air Service, both of which are outside the remit of this book. Churchill's instructions for the creation of the Glider Pilot Regiment, together with some operational records, can be found in WO 233.

The use of gliders was abandoned soon after the end of the Second World War and the Glider Pilot Regiment was disbanded in 1957. The Army Air Corps was disbanded in 1950, but the need for an Army corps to be responsible for aviation led to the Army Air Corps being re-formed at the same time as the Glider Pilot Regiment was disbanded. Records concerning the Army Air Corps can be found in WO 295.

4 ROYAL ENGINEERS BALLOON SECTION RECORDS OF SERVICE

The records discussed in this chapter concern the personnel of the RE Balloon Section, its forebears and successors up to 12 May 1912 only. Records of service of the RFC, RNAS and RAF are dealt with in chapters 5, 6 and 7 respectively.

4.1 Officers

The first type of record to approach when researching any officers who served in the British Army after 1760 is the *Army Lists*. These lists are available in the Open Reading Room. They appear in a variety of formats (yearly, half yearly, quarterly and monthly), each with its own particular type of information. Each volume is internally indexed, with the number alongside the name representing a page reference within the volume. In many cases officers may appear on more than one page, especially if they are of senior rank. The *Army Lists* contain gradation lists arranged in order of seniority, i.e. date of promotion to a given rank. These can provide more information about appointments and courses attended. The 'War Services' sections provide brief details about the military operations an officer was involved in, together with information about medals and awards.

Also of use, although not officially created by the state, are *Hart's Army Lists* 1879–1915. These lists contain information which is not readily available in the 'official' *Army List*. The biographical papers created by Hart covering the period 1838–75 and relating to many of the officers found in these lists can be found in WO 211. *Hart's Army Lists* are available in the Open Reading Room and Library.

A published list of RE officers, the *Roll of Officers of the Corps of Royal Engineers from 1660–1898*, is available in the Library.

Records of service of RE officers kept by the War Office can be found in WO 25/3913–3920; information within these records covers the period 1796–1937. These records are arranged by date of commission and they contain biographical data concerning both the officer and, if he had them, his wife and children, including dates of promotions and appointments, campaigns and medals, and his nominated next of kin.

Reference	Date
wo 25/3913	1796–1860
wo 25/3914	1860–1921
wo 25/3915	1873–1928
wo 25/3916	1886–1918
wo 25/3917	1885–1937
wo 25/3918	1895–1935
wo 25/3919	1904–1915
wo 25/3920	1876–1915 (includes the RE Supplementary Reserve)

Records of service formerly held by the Royal Engineers can be found in wo 76/15–23. These records cover the period 1866–1907 and are arranged by Royal Engineer division, with each volume internally indexed. However, these records only concern RE (Militia) (part-time) officers.

WAR OFFICE: RECORDS OF OFFICERS' SERVICE, ROYAL ENGINEERS (M)

Reference	Date	Division
wo 76/15	1879–1907	Falmouth
wo 76/16	1880–1906	Harwich
wo 76/17	1872–1897	Harwich
wo 76/18	1892–1906	Humber
wo 76/19	1866–1905	Medway
wo 76/20	1882–1906	Milford Haven
wo 76/21	1874–1906	Plymouth
wo 76/22	1896–1905	Thames
wo 76/23	1888–1904	Western

4.2 Other Ranks

As the Royal Engineers did not embark upon experiments with balloons until 1878, the records of service of men involved in pioneering British military aviation are scarce. Although the process to find such records is easy, in many cases, unless you know that an individual serving in the Royal Engineers was involved in ballooning, then the outward signs on a record of service do not necessarily help.

The records of service of those men of the British Army who were discharged to pension up to 1913, who or served on a short service engagement which expired between 1883 and 1913, are in the record series wo 97. These records are arranged in chronological sections covering 1873–82, 1883–1900 and 1900–13; each section is arranged in alphabetical order.

Prior to 1883 each chronological section is arranged by regiment or corps. After 1883 each chronological section represents the whole Army and is not broken into regimental or corps groups. The piece ranges of the sections are:

Date	Reference	Coverage
1873–1882	WO 97/1849–1857	Specifically Royal Engineers
1883–1900	WO 97/2172–4231	All of the Army
1900–1913	WO 97/4232–6322	All of the Army
1900–1913	WO 97/6323–6354	Supplementary series
1843–1899	WO 97/6355–6383	Supplementary series

The records in this series are likely to provide some of the following information:

Physical description at attestation and discharge
Date of attestation and discharge
Dates of promotions
Medical and disciplinary histories
Dates of overseas and campaign service
Details about medals
Name of wife and children (if any), together with marriage and baptism dates
Intended place of residence on discharge.

4.3 Case Studies

Case studies cannot cover all of the permutations of service. The following examples illustrate what information can be found in the resources available.

4.3.1 Gerard Moore Heath

Gerard Heath was born on 7 June 1863, son of Admiral Sir Leopold and Mary Heath. After being educated at Wimbledon and the Royal Military Academy, Woolwich, he was commissioned into the Royal Engineers in February 1882. In a career that was to last until 1919, it was as early as 1884 that Heath encountered balloons with his participation in the Bechuanaland operations.

Promoted to Captain in 1890, Heath went on to see further operational service in India in 1895. Gaining his majority on 4 October 1899, he soon sailed with a large part of the British Army to South Africa. It was in South Africa, specifically during the defence of Ladysmith, that Heath was reacquainted with balloons by commanding the balloon section which was part of the besieged garrison.

For his service in South Africa, Heath was given a brevet promotion to

Fig. 8 (facing)
The Royal Engineer officer's record of service of G. M. Heath. WO 25/3915

26 · *Royal Engineers Balloon Section Records of Service*

STATEMENT of the Services of _Gerard Moore Heath_ of the _Royal Engineers_

Where Born _Holmwood, Surrey_ Date of Birth _7th June 1863_ Age on his

with a Record of such other Particulars as may be useful in case of his Death.

his entrance into the Army _(18 years 9 months_ Religious Persuasion _Church of England_

Ranks.	FULL PAY.		HALF PAY,	Dates.
	Full Pay.	Half Pay.		
Lieutenant Roy Eng⁹				12 Jan'y Noted 1882
Captain	—do—			Feb'y 90
Major	—do—			3 Aug 98
				4 Oct 99
Lieut. Colonel Brevet				22 Aug 02
Lieut. Colonel R.E.				16 Aug 04
Colonel Brevet				20 Aug 07
Colonel (Substantive)				18 Aug 11
Brig. General (Temp)				16 Oct 14

SERVICE AT HOME.

Period.			Stations.
From.	To.	Yrs. Days.	

SERVICE ABROAD.

Period.			Stations.
From.	To.	Yrs. Days.	

Titles, Honorary Distinctions, and Medals obtained, and if conferred for any specified Service, appointed for what occasion.

D.S.O.

C.B.

List and Dates of any Battles, Sieges, and Campaigns in which the Officer was present, specifying the Regimental or Staff Situation he held on each occasion, and the Name of the Officer in Chief Command.

Bechuanaland Expedition 1885, as Lieutenant

S.African War 1899 to 1902

Name and Residence of the Officer's Next of Kin, according to the legal ties of Consanguinity.
(To be inserted with particular care.)

Name.	Degree of Relationship.	Latest known Place of Residence.			Street and No.
		County.	Parish.	Town.	
	Uncle		Surrey	Capel	Dorking	Anstie Grange Holmwood
Leopold Gittatt Heath	Father		Surrey	Capel	Dorking	Anstie Grange
Mary Heath	Wife				With husband	

If the Officer be Married, specify

When.	Where.	To whom.	The Wife living at the Date of	Minister who Married the Parties, and of what Church.
1893	Odd Rode Cheshire	Mary Egerton		

18 August

If the Officer has any Legitimate Children, specify

Names.	Dates of Birth.	Where Baptised.

Lieutenant Colonel and made a Companion of the Distinguished Service Order.

Promoted to full Lieutenant Colonel in 1906, postings to India and Burma were followed in 1912 by a return to South Africa as Temporary Brigadier-General, General Staff.

During the First World War, Heath served initially as Inspector of Royal Engineers, followed by appointment as Chief Engineer, First Army and promotion to Temporary Major-General in November 1915. Promotion to substantive Major-General for distinguished service in the field followed and he was appointed Engineer-in-Chief to the British armies in the field in November 1917, an appointment he was to hold until the end of the war.

Heath was further decorated for his services during the war by being made a Companion of the Most Honourable Order of the Bath (CB) in 1916 and he was knighted in 1919, when he was made a Knight Commander of the Most Distinguished Order of St Michael and St George (KCMG). Sir Gerard Moore Heath, KCMG, CB, DSO, RE, retired from the Army in December 1919, and died in January 1929.

The records of service of G.M. Heath can be found in WO 25/3915 and WO 374/32333. A copy of Heath's record in WO 25/3915 can be seen in Fig. 8.

4.3.2 Charles Robertson

Charles Robertson was born in Lambeth, Surrey, in 1867 and joined the Royal Engineers as a bugler, aged 14, in 1881. From his record of service there is no outward sign that Charles was ever involved with balloons. It is only when you delve deeper that a connection with aviation appears.

On enlistment Robertson was described as 5' ¾" tall, with a fair complexion, blue eyes and brown hair. After attending a telegraphy course in November 1882, home service continued, with little to report.

Promoted to Sapper in 1884, he left the country for his first overseas posting to Egypt and the Sudan on 16 February 1885. On this first journey overseas, Robertson was also to see his only active service, around the Red Sea port of Suakin, which resulted in him receiving the Egypt Medal with Suakin 1885 clasp and Khedive's Star 1884–6. It was whilst verifying these medals that the connection with the RE Balloon Section was confirmed by his appearance on their medal roll in WO 100/64 ff81.

Robertson returned to England in July 1885, and another course in telegraphy is noted in November 1887. With this new qualification, promotion to Lance Corporal followed in January 1887, to Second Corporal in May 1887 and then to Corporal and Sergeant in May and December, respectively, both in the year 1888.

During this period of home service, Charles Robertson married Florence Jane Davis at Holy Trinity Church, Plymouth, on 15 February 1892. Two

Fig. 9, 10 (facing and following page) *The record of service of Charles Robertson who spent most of his army career in the RE Balloon Section.* WO 97/5790

ATTESTATION OF

Army Form B. 267.

No. *16900* Name *Charles Robertson*

Corps *Royal Engineers*

Joined at *London*

on *29 January 1881*

H. Ellice
Col

For Twelve Years Army Service.

Questions to be put to the Recruit before Enlistment.

1. What is your Name?	*Charles Robertson*
2. In or near what Parish or Town were you born?	In the Parish of *Lambeth*, in or near the Town of *London* is the County of *Surrey*
3. What is your Age?	*17* Years, ... Months.
4. What is your Trade or Calling?	*Musician*
5. Are you, or have you been, an Apprentice? if so, where? to whom? and for what period?	*No*
6. Have you resided out of your Father's house, and paid rates and taxes of £10 value, and if so, where?	*No*
7. Are you Married?	*No*
8. Have you ever been discharged with Ignominy, or as Incorrigible and Worthless, from the Regular Forces, or from any portion of the Auxiliary Forces when subject to Military Law, or from the Reserve Forces, or have you been dismissed with disgrace from the Navy? And you are warned that there is a special provision in the Army Discipline and Regulation Act which renders you liable to Penal Servitude if you are convicted of making a false answer to this question.	*No*
‡ 9. Do you now belong to, or have you ever served in, any Regiment, Brigade, or Corps in Her Majesty's Army?	*No*
‡10. Do you now belong to, or have you ever served in, the Marines?	*No*
‡11. Do you now belong to, or have you ever served in, the Militia, or Militia Reserve?	*No*
‡ 12. Do you now belong to, or have you ever served in, the Royal Navy?	*No*
13. Do you now belong to the Volunteers, or to the Naval Coast Volunteers? or to the Royal Naval Reserve Force?	*No*
‡ If so, the Recruit is to state the particulars of his former Service, and the cause of his Discharge, and is to produce, if possible, his Parchment Certificate of Discharge.	
14. Have you truly stated the whole, if any, of your previous Service?	*Yes*
15. Have you ever been rejected as unfit for Her Majesty's Service?	*No*
16. For what Corps are you willing to be enlisted, or are you willing to be enlisted for General Service?	For *Royal Engineers*
17. Did you receive a Notice, and do you understand its meaning?	*Yes*
18. Who gave you the Notice?	*Staff Sergt Major Hunter*
19. Are you willing to serve for the term of twelve Years, provided Her Majesty should so long require your services.	*Yes*
20. Are you willing to serve for a further term, not exceeding twelve months, if beyond the sea, or if a state of War exists between Her Majesty and any Foreign power, if you should be directed so to serve by the Secretary of State for War, or by the Commanding Officer on any Foreign Colonial or Indian station, or any competent Military Authority?	*Yes*

I, *Charles Robertson* do solemnly declare that the above answers made by me to the above questions are true and that I am willing to fulfil the engagement made.

(Sd) *Charles Robertson* {Signature of Recruit} (Sd) *S. E. Endacott Sergt* {Signature of Witness}

OATH TO BE TAKEN BY RECRUIT ON ATTESTATION.

I, *Charles Robertson* do make Oath, that I will be faithful and bear true Allegiance to Her Majesty, Her Heirs, and Successors, and that I will, as in duty bound, honestly and faithfully defend Her Majesty, Her Heirs, and Successors, in Person, Crown, and Dignity, against all enemies, and will observe and obey all orders of Her Majesty, Her Heirs, and Successors, and of the Generals and Officers set over me, So help me God.

Witness my hand.

Signature of Recruit (Sd) *Charles Robertson*

Witness present (Sd) *S. E. Endacott Sgt*

CERTIFICATE OF MAGISTRATE.

The Recruit above-named was cautioned by me that if he made any false answer to any of the above questions he would be liable to be punished as provided in the Army Discipline and Regulation Act.

The above questions were then read to the recruit in my presence.

I have taken care that he understands each question, and that his answer to each question has been duly received as directed, and the said recruit has made and signed the declaration and oath before me at *Wohns police Ct* on this *29* day of *January* one thousand eight hundred and eighty *one*

Signature of the Justice (Sd) *L. T. d'Eyncourt*

The Recruit should, if he require it, receive a copy of the Declaration.

For Authority Boys R 137 *22.1.81* (Sd) *J. P. Prevost Co*

Service at Home and Abroad.

Country.	From.	To.	Years	Days.	The Country only to be shown —it is not neces-sary to show separately the service in the dif-ferent stations of same country.
Home	29th Jan 81	15·2·85	4	18	
Egypt	16·2·85	7·7·85		142	
Home	8·7·85	4·6·94	8	331	
Halifax NS	5·6·94	28·11·97	3	178	
Home	29·11·97	28·1·06	8	61	
			25	0	

NOTE.—For mode of computing Foreign Service, see G. O. 56 of 1874.

		Initials of Officer making the Entry.
Next of Kin	mother Sarah. Brothers. Andrew, Thomas & George. Sisters Margaret, Sarah, Mary, Alice & Louisa. Wife with him	
Campaigns.	Egyptian (Suakin) 1885	
Wounded.	Nil	mc. Capt. RE.
Effects of Wounds.		
Special instances of gal-lant conduct		
Medals and decorations	Medal "Egypt" & Clasp Suakin 1885 Khedives Bronze Star 1884 & 86 Long Service and Good Conduct June 1899	
Injuries in or by the Service	Nil	mc. Capt. RE.
Married — To whom, Place and Date	With leave to Florence Jane Davis at Holy Trinity Church Plymouth 15·2·99	Capt RE
Passed Classes of In-struction	Telegraphy "Very Good" 24·11·82 Telegraphy (5th) "Superior" 6·11·86 Hythe Certificate for Musketry 30·11·91	
Certificates of Education	3d Class 29/7 80. 2d 6/7 81. 1 Cl. 31/36	
Character on being passed to Reserve	Names of Children Dates of Birth	
Character on being Dis-charged	Gladys Florence 29–11–93 Charles Stuart 31–1–94	Capt RE
Place of Discharge		
Cause of Discharge		
Pension awarded		
Died		
Notes	£ 52–10–6 Deferred Pay issued on 28·1·02	

NOTE.—These entries are to be made from time to time as they occur, and initialed by the Officer making the entry.

children were born before Robertson's next overseas posting: Gladys Florence on 29 November 1892 and Charles Stewart on 31 January 1894. The birth of Charles Stewart Robertson occurred just before his father went on his second and last overseas posting, a two-and-a-half year spell of garrison duty in Halifax, Nova Scotia. Shortly after his arrival in Halifax, Sergeant Robertson was promoted to Company Sergeant Major on 1 July 1894.

Returning to England on 29 November 1897, his final promotion, to Quarter Master Sergeant, occurred on 8 March 1898.

Quarter Master Sergeant Charles Robertson, RE, was finally discharged from the Army on 28 January 1906. His appearance was very similar to that when he enlisted, but he was now 5'8"! His intended place of residence on discharge was 27 Anson Place, St Judes, Plymouth. Charles Robertson died on 1 July 1951, aged 84, at Gillingham in Kent.

All of this detail came from his record of service in WO 97/5790, which can be seen in Fig. 9 and Fig. 10.

4.3.3   William McEwen

Born in Coylton, Ayrshire, in 1855, William McEwen joined the Royal Engineers aged 24 years and 2 months on 15 April 1879.

How McEwen became involved with balloons is not revealed by his record of service, but by 1885 he was serving with the Balloon Detachment at Suakin in the Sudan. For his service in the Sudan, McEwen was awarded the Egypt Medal with Suakin 1885 clasps and the Khedive's Star 1884–6, and this is recorded in WO 100/64 folio 81.

McEwen's experience with the RE Balloon Section was further strengthened in 1888 when he was sent on a balloon course at the School of Military Engineering. The assessment of McEwen on the balloon course was recorded on his record of service as 'Very Superior'.

Although there is nothing on McEwen's record of service to indicate any postings away from the RE Balloon Section, his involvement with balloons in the Sudan and his attendance on the balloon course in 1888 would indicate a career 'balloonatic'!

William McEwen was awarded the Army Long Service and Good Conduct Medal in 1897. Continuing with the Balloon Section, William McEwen saw further operational service with No.2 Balloon Section in South Africa during the Boer War. For his service in South Africa Company Sergeant Major William McEwen was awarded the Queen's South Africa Medal with the clasp Natal and South Africa 1901.

After a pioneering career with the RE Balloon Section Company, Sergeant Major William McEwen was pensioned from the Army at Aldershot on 16 April 1901 with his intended place of residence being 162 Queens Road in Aldershot.

William McEwen's record of service can be found in WO 97/5403.

5 ROYAL FLYING CORPS RECORDS OF SERVICE

The records discussed in this chapter are primarily those created and held by the War Office and are concerned with service prior to the formation of the Royal Air Force on 1 April 1918. There are, however, a number of references to Air Ministry Records in AIR 1, though that ministry was not in existence at the outbreak of the First World War.

5.1 Officers

The Royal Flying Corps was a corps of the British Army and therefore officers were either commissioned into another regiment or corps and then transferred in, or they were commissioned directly into the RFC.

As with all commissioned officers of all three services, basic details about commissions and promotions can be obtained from the *Army Lists*. Officers of the RFC (Military Wing) and RFC appear in the *Army Lists* from 1912 until 1919.

Immediate pre-First World War records of service for RFC officers who left the service prior to the outbreak of the First World War do not exist. If he joined another regiment or corps prior to transfer, there is a possibility that an incomplete record of service covering an officer's initial (i.e. pre-RFC) service may be found in WO 25 or WO 76. The majority of RFC officers' records of service are to be found in the record series WO 339 and WO 374.

5.1.1 WO 339 and WO 374

The records in these two War Office record series are arranged in different ways. WO 339 is arranged by War Office 'Long Number' (unique identifying number), while WO 374 is arranged alphabetically.

In order to obtain the 'Long Number' for use with WO 339, it is necessary to consult the index of Officers' Long Numbers in WO 338.

WO 338 consists of 23 indexes that are available on microfilm in the Open Reading Room. WO 338/1–21 consists of an alphabetical index of officers who were commissioned from 1901–20. WO 338/22 is the name index of officers commissioned between 1871 and 1901.

Fig. 11 (facing)
Nominal roll of first 55 pilots of RFC.
AIR 1/686/21/13/2252

Area (H) 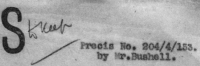 Precis No. 204/4/153.
by Mr.Bushell.

Subject:- R.F.C. Pilots available in England on August 17th 1914.

Dates covered   August 17th, 1914.

R.F.C. (M.W.) File.

The O.C., R.F.C., (M.W.) S. FARNBOROUGH, forwarded to the
D.C. of M.A., War Office, a list of Fifty-five Pilots available
to fly machines, pointing out that some of these officers were
not sufficiently advanced to fly across country.   The names and
rank of the fifty-five Pilots is appended :-

Rank.	Name.
Bt. Major, O.C.	W.H.Trenchard.
Squadron Commander.	J.H.W.Becke.
Major.	W.H.S.Burch.
Flight Commander.	W.Picton Warlow.
"	E.G.Harvey.
"	F.T.Holt.
"	R.Pigot.
"	B.R.W.Beor.
"	C.Fox.
"	G.B.Stopford.
"	G.de Havilland.
Flying Officers.	H.F.Glanville.
"	R.O.Abercromby.
"	B.C.Hucks.
Captain.	E.W.Furse.
Captain.	L.F.Evans.
Flying Officer.	F.St.G.Tucker.
"	H.C.Mac Donnell.
"	R.E.Lewis.
"	F.B.Binney.
"	R.C.Bewes.
"	P.A.Broder.
"	R.L.Charteris.
"	C.H.Marks.
"	E.L.K.Davis.
"	Hon.E.A.Stonor.
"	H.S.Keating.
"	C.M.Griffiths.
"	H.C.T.Dowding.
"	H.C.Barber.
"	A.M.Wynne.
"	E.F.Norris.
"	Adams.
"	J.Valentine.
"	R.Lorraine.
"	T.F.Rutledge.
"	L.Parker.
"	J.G.Miller.
"	J.R.Howett.
"	R.Orr-Paterson.
"	M.B.Blake.
"	A.Payze.
"	C.B.Rickards.
"	T.H.Leveson-Gower.
"	A.V.Bettington.
"	H.C.Tower.
"	C.C.Gold.
"	A.B.Forde
"	W.H.Charlesworth.
"	A.B.Bagley.
"	Joubert.
"	C.F.Lee.
"	Corbett Wilson.
"	Astford.
"	Moorhouse

Each index is arranged in five columns giving: surname, forename/initial(s), regiment/corps, 'long number', rank. The regiment or corps an officer served in is indicated either by abbreviations for corps or by pre-1882 numerical regimental designator. In many cases the numerical reference may be made up to two numbers by a '/'. The first number is the battalion and the second number the regiment. Thus, 7/45 is the 7th Battalion, Notts and Derby Regiment (Sherwood Foresters). Details relating to regimental numbers can be found in the *Army List*.

In many cases the references found in WO 338 appear in a different form from the purely numerical. If a file reference is prefixed with a 'P', the file is still retained by the Ministry of Defence. If a file reference is prefixed by the first letter of the surname, the first vowel of the surname, and a number, the file may survive in WO 374.

Once you have obtained the 'Long Number' of the officer whose record is being sought, you need to look that number up in the WO 339 series list. The 'Long Number' is the number on the right-hand side of the page, with the WO 339 piece number being on the left. If you use the online lists, to identify the 'Long Number' click on the 'Details' icon to show the original reference (the 'Long Number').

WO 374, which is arranged alphabetically, contains the records of service of officers commissioned into the Territorial Army, as well as many files of officers who had been commissioned prior to 1901 and who had retired before the First World War but were recalled.

5.1.2 AIR 1

Although the records in AIR 1 were deposited at the National Archives by the Air Ministry, many were originally created by the RFC when it was a corps of the British Army. There are numerous files containing details about RFC officers, arranged both by unit and under general headings. Subjects include:

Roll of officers of the RFC with the BEF, 4–30 August 1914	AIR 1/2442/305/18/8
Chart of Air Service Officers	AIR 1/2530
Posting of officers after completion of course at Central Flying School, 1913–15	AIR 1/787/204/4/609
Names of officers for promotion examination, July–August 1914	AIR 1/764/204/4/225
Nominal roll of officers, NCOs and men who proceeded to France, August 1914	AIR 1/765/204/4/237
Seniority roll of RFC officers, July 1914	AIR 1/774/204/4/364

There are numerous files concerning officers' correspondence, personal reports, details relating to next of kin, etc. Most of these files are arranged under unit headings.

Fig. 12 (facing) Officers and SE 5a Scouts of No 1 Squadron, RAF at Clairmarais aerodrome near Ypres, Belgium.

5.2 Airmen

Although AIR 79 contains the records of service of men of the RFC, the War Office did keep a number of records of service of men of the RFC who were discharged from the service before the RAF was formed. These are described in the following sections.

5.2.1 WO 97

The records of men who were discharged before the end of 1913 are in the record series WO 97. This series is arranged alphabetically. For further details about this series see 4.2.

5.2.2 WO 363 and WO 364

The majority of records of service of other ranks who saw service in the First World War were destroyed by enemy action (a fire at the War Office

repository) on 6/7 September 1940. The surviving records, arranged in two record series (WO 363 and WO 364), are available on microfilm and online.

WO 363 contains records of men who survived the war, who were killed in action, died of wounds or disease, who were executed, or who were discharged from the service for other reasons. The records in this series, known as the 'Burnt Records', were microfilmed with the help of a generous grant from the Heritage Lottery Fund.

The records in WO 363 may contain attestation and discharge data, details of physique, medical and conduct records, details of next of kin and details of promotions, postings and overseas service. As these records are those that survived both fire and water damage, their physical quality is very poor.

After the Second World War, the War Office put the surviving records into an alphabetical sequence and appealed to other government departments holding records relating to servicemen who had seen service in the First World War to return them to the War Office to replace the records lost in 1940. The majority of the returned records came from the Ministry of Pensions and primarily related to men who had been discharged from the Army as a result of sickness or wounds contracted or received between 1914 and 1920.

Beyond the normal type of military data found in WO 97 or WO 363, the records in WO 364 contain detailed medical records relating to the reasons why an individual was discharged from the Army. It is also possible to find numerous records of pre-First World War pensioners who returned to the colours in 1914, and who, although they did not see service overseas, did see service in the United Kingdom. Thus, in WO 364, it is possible to find men of the RFC and former members of the RE Balloon Section.

The digitization of WO 363 and WO 364 has now been carried out by *Ancestry.co.uk*, and access is freely available at the National Archives or remotely to subscribers via the *Ancestry.co.uk* website.

The great advantage of digitizing the content of WO 363 and WO 364 is that each individual has been itemized. It is therefore possible to search by name, estimated or known year of birth, and by service details such as regiment/corps and number.

5.3 Case Studies

Artefacts such as medals, personal papers or a memorial plaque can provide a useful starting point when researching a military career, even if the individual died in service.

5.3.1 Alan Geoffrey Fox

The case of A.G. Fox illustrates the fact that an end can be a beginning to a research project.

The next of kin of all those men and women who died up to seven years after the end of the First World War as a result of war service received a bronze Memorial Plaque (see Fig. 13). The medal was given whether they were killed in action, died of wounds or disease or in an accident whilst on military service. Sometimes known as the 'Death Plaque' or 'Dead Man's Penny', the Memorial Plaque, which was cast in bronze, contains the name, usually in full, of the person it commemorates. Many plaques are of course identical; how many John Smiths died in the war?

A name search on the Commonwealth War Graves Commission (CWGC) website (*www.cwgc.org*) showed only one Alan Geoffrey Fox as having died during the First World War. (This search could also have been done by contacting the CWGC in writing—see 15.7.) The plaque for Alan Geoffrey Fox is thus unique.

The CWGC describes Fox as one of the first five officers in the Army taught to fly. In the history of British military aviation Fox is obviously very important.

Alan Geoffrey Fox was born in London on 6 November 1887, son of Charles James and Beatrice Clara Fox. He was commissioned as Second Lieutenant in the Royal Engineers in February 1908.

Little is known of Fox's career before 1910. However, in the July 1914 *Army List*, he is shown as having joined the Royal Engineers Balloon

Fig. 13 *The First World War Memorial Plaque of Alan Geoffrey Fox.*

School in February 1910, and being promoted to Lieutenant (Lt) in July of the same year. The creation of the Air Battalion, Royal Engineers and his transfer to it in April 1911 are also noted. The subsequent creation of the Royal Flying Corps and Fox's transfer to it on 13 May 1912 are also shown.

As Fox was one of the founding pilots of the RFC, the chance of finding documents relating to him in AIR 1 was very high. A roll of officers of the RFC from May 1912 to August 1913 in AIR 1/803/204/4/1158 shows the following:

Lt. Temporary Captain Fox, A.G.
Promoted Lt 30 July 1910
Promoted Captain (Capt.) Temporary 20 October 1912
Date of Royal Aero Club Certificate No.176, 30 January 1912,
    with Special Certificate No.5 (to fly airships) 16 July 1912
Date of Gazette to Military Wing RFC 13 May 1912
Currently employed as Flight Commander No.3 squadron

Fig. 14 *Sqdn RFC summary of work recording the loss of Capt A. G. Fox.* AIR 1/253/204/8/9

Just after the outbreak of the First World War, the Royal Flying Corps carried out a survey of the aircraft types its pilots could fly. So great was the ability of Fox that he was noted as being able to fly any machine (AIR 1/761/204/4/153).

PAGE.1.   SUMMARY OF WORK.   R.F.C. Form No. 302.

No.16   Squadron, Royal Flying Corps.   Date   9th May.   1915

Type	Pilot	Observer	Duty	Hour of Departure	Hour of Return	Remarks
B.E2c. 1752	2/Lt.Walker	Lt.James	Attempted Reconnaissance	4.am	4.20am	Unsuccessful owing to strong wind.
-:- -:-	-:-	Capt.Cairnes	Reconnaissance	12.35pm	2.5.pm	1.Copy of report to 1st Army,2 copies to 1st Advanced Wing.
BE2a 388	Lt.Cunningham.	Lieut.James	Reconnaissance.	6.50am	8.25am	1.copy of report to 1st Army, 2 copies to 1st Advanced Wing.
Voisin 1877	Capt.Fox.	Nil	Bomb dropping as ordered	3.am		Did not return.
-:- 1879	Lt.Glanville.	Nil	Bomb Dropping as ordered	3.am	4.45am	Bombs dropped. (Pilot wounded during journey.)
-:- 1879	Lt.Braithwaite	Nil	Testing Machine.	3.45pm	4.0pm	Satisfactory.
-:- 1868	Lt.Eberli.	Lt.Sanford.	Reconnaissance.	3.50am		Have not yet returned.
MF. 1853	Capt.Porter	Capt.Bradley	Wireless Tactical Observation.	5.am	7.25am	Successful
,, -:-	-:-	-:-	-:- -:-	8.45am	11.30am	-:-
,, 1869	Lt.Grattan-Bellew	Lt.Gordon.	-:- -:-	7.30am	9.30am	-:-
,, 1857	Lt.MacDonald	Capt.Howell.	-:- -:-	6.20am	8.am	-:-
,, 757	-:-	-:-	-:- -:-	1.50pm	4.25pm	-:-
,, 1869	Lt.Grattan-Bellew	Lt.Gorden. -	-:- -:-	4.pm	6.25pm	-:-
BE2c. 1676	Capt.Playfair	Lt.Coventry	Attempted Reconnaissance	5.35pm	7.pm	Unsuccessful. Engine failed at BAILLEUL
Voisin 1879	Lt.Braithwaite	2/Lt.Holmes	Reconnaissance	4.50pm	7.5pm	1 copy of report to 1st Army, 2 copies to 1st Advanced Wing

Major.R.F.C.
O.C.No.16.Squadron.R.F.C.

W 13040—965 5000 3/15 H W V(P). H 15/391

Travelling to France on 29 August 1914, Fox joined the RFC Aircraft Park but returned to England in mid-September. Returning to France on 24 October 1914, this time he joined a squadron, 5 Squadron, rather than serving at the Aircraft Park. On an unknown date Fox left 5 Squadron and joined the unit, 16 Squadron, he was to serve in until his death.

The work summary of 16 Squadron, in AIR 1/1253/204/8/9, records just two flights carried out by Fox. The first flight, on 3 May 1915, was a reconnaissance flight, but it was unsuccessful owing to a leaking radiator. The second and last operational flight by Alan Geoffrey Fox whilst serving with 16 Squadron was also to be his last.

Taking off in Voisin no.1877 at 3.00 a.m. on 9 May 1915, Fox's task was to bomb a bridge over the Le Bassee-Dom canal. According to the squadron work summary, he failed to return (see Fig. 14). Interestingly, there is an Aircraft Log Book (AIR 1/2070/204/412/1877) for the plane Fox flew on his last operational flight, and it is one of a number of sources in AIR 1 which provide details of the circumstances of his death and subsequent burial. The Aircraft Log Book notes that Fox took off with two 100-pound bombs (these would have slowed the plane down considerably) and that he was brought down between the German and French lines. The plane was burnt by bombs thrown from the German trenches. Captain Fox's body was recovered at night by the French and buried at Cambrin. Another report in AIR 1 actually records the names of the French soldiers who recovered his body (AIR 1/1254/204/8/29). So ended the life, at the age of 27, of one of the RFC's most able pilots.

Fox's records of service can be found in WO 339/7034 and AIR 76/168. His career can be further expanded upon by looking at the numerous AIR 1 references quoted in the text.

5.3.2 *Claude Vincent Abbott*

The digitization of WO 363 and WO 364 means that it is possible to search by regiment as well as name. For those interested in finding the records of service for men of a particular unit, unit searching is a great advance!

There are around the world many photographs of men in military uniform from the First World War period. Many of these photographs show men whose identity is unknown, but the photographs in the hands of families will hopefully have at least a list of possible subject individuals if not the full details of the subject.

During the First World War it was not unusual for men to be transferred voluntarily or compulsorily to another unit. In such cases, if the transfer is unknown to the researcher, finding a record of service can be problematic.

Claude Vincent Abbott attested for the Royal Flying Corps on 10 December 1915, just before conscription came into force. On attestation

Vincent was living at 10 Woodville Grove, Woodhouse Lane, Leeds, and his occupation was photographer.

Transferred to the Army Reserve on the same day as his attestation, Abbott was eventually mobilized on 21 November 1916. Abbott arrived at the RFC depot at Farnborough on 23 November 1916, where he was allocated the RFC number of 50090.

Very little is known about Abbott's RFC career after November 1916. Suffice it to say his photographic skills were needed by another section of the Army, for on 3 March 1917 he was compulsorily transferred to the Army Service Corps for duty with the Army Printing and Stationery Service (APSS) as a photographer!

Posted to France as S/300860 Private C.V. Abbott ASC on 13 March 1917, Abbott arrived at the APSS depot in Boulogne on the same day. After a further posting to No.3 Advanced Section APSS at St Pol on 26 April 1917, Abbott was moved around the APSS in France, with postings to No.4 Advanced Section at Dunkirk in the summer of 1917 and then to APSS at GHQ in Italy in January 1918.

Claude Abbott was eventually demobilized from the Army Service Corps on 11 March 1919.

6 ROYAL NAVAL AIR SERVICE RECORDS OF SERVICE

The records of service of men of the RNAS within the ADM record series contain details of officers and men who, for example, joined the Royal Navy and subsequently transferred into the RNAS, as well as of those who joined the Royal Naval Air Service at any time after its creation, up to 31 March 1918. The records of service of men of the RNAS who transferred into the RAF are discussed in chapter 7.

6.1 Officers

Officers serving in the Royal Naval Air Service either transferred in from other branches of the Royal Navy or joined it directly. Thus, records of service for officers of the RNAS may be found in two different record series (ADM 196 and ADM 273), which are described in the following sections.

6.1.1 ADM 196

The records in ADM 196 consist of single-sheet records of service for officers who were commissioned into the Royal Navy prior to 1908 and who subsequently specialized in aviation. The majority of the records for officers who specialized in aviation are in ADM 196/42–56, with an index in ADM 196/57. The index is not completely reliable because many of the individuals mentioned in it have no records of service. Much of ADM 196/57 has been transcribed into a card index which has converted the original index into TNA references. This card index is available in the Open Reading Room.

Records of service in ADM 196 provide date and place of birth, date of commission, the names of ships served upon, promotions, name of next of kin, details of wife and children as appropriate, and brief notes from confidential reports.

For officers promoted to the rank of Captain and above there is a further collection of records within the same series. These are arranged by date of promotion (seniority) to Captain.

ADM 196/86–94 contains the records of service of officers of the rank of Captain and above. Arranged by seniority, they cover the period 1893–1944 and therefore include records of officers who did not transfer to the RAF on its formation, and who may eventually have seen service with the Fleet Air Arm.

6.1.2   ADM 273

ADM 273 contains records of service of both commissioned and warrant officers and consists of the records of men who joined the RNAS after its formation in July 1914. This series consists of 30 volumes, each of which is internally indexed. There is a complete card index to this series in the Open Reading Room. However, the contents of this card index have been entered into the Catalogue, where it is now possible to search ADM 273 by the name of the officer. Any search results will provide the exact ADM 273 reference down to page level.

It is possible for an officer to be found in more than one volume of ADM 273. Most of the volumes cross-refer to other entries, as does the index. For example, a search for Arthur Bedward Spencer produces ADM 273/7/74, ADM 273/23/311 and ADM 273/30/133. The last elements of these references are the page numbers. Therefore, when ordering an ADM 273 you only need to use the elements ADM 273/7. Do not include the page number.

The records in this series can provide date and place of birth, date of commission and promotions, details of postings and brief notes from confidential reports.

6.1.3   ADM 1

As with the RFC, there are a large number of records in ADM 1 which concern RNAS officers. Most of the files concerning RNAS officers are either collected under the Admiralty section within the series, or under the records of given units. Amongst the general files are:

List of naval officers selected for aeronautical service, 1912	AIR 1/649/17/122/400
Disposition lists of RNAS officers, showing where they were serving at a given date, April 1914–September 1918	AIR 1/2108/207/49/1–1/2110/207/49/9
A list of those officers of the RNAS who served in the Gallipoli campaign, April 1915–January 1916	AIR 1/675/21/13/1563
Weekly return of officers and ratings at RNAS station Roehampton and Kite balloon sections abroad, 1917	AIR 1/447/15/303/40

6.2   Ratings

Although the main collection of records of service for ratings is ADM 188, details concerning men of the RNAS Armoured Car Units can also be found elsewhere.

The series ADM 188 has been digitized and placed on DocumentsOnline, where it is possible to search by name and/or official number. If you find an appropriate record of service, it is possible to download it. Downloading away from the National Archives building requires the payment of a fee.

6.2.1   ADM 188

The information contained in an ADM 188 includes date and place of birth, date of enlistment, physical description and the names of ships and dates served on those ships.

Many ships used by the Royal Naval Air Service and later the Fleet Air Arm were, and still are, concrete or non-seagoing frigates, i.e. shore bases, airfields and other establishments. The best source for knowing if a ship listed in an RN record of service went to sea is to consult *Shore Establishments of the Royal Navy* by Ben Warlow.

The record series ADM 188 contains the records of service of all naval ratings who served at any time between 1873 and 1923. This series holds the records of men whose service encompassed the year 1873, when this particular series of records started, right up to men who enlisted in 1923. The Royal Navy changed its record keeping again in 1929, and therefore the records of men who saw service after 1928 contain little further detail beyond noting the date on which they qualified for their Long Service and Good Conduct Medals (see 10.10.2) or the date of death if they were a Second World War casualty.

The Royal Navy changed its service number format twice between 1873 and 1914. Between 1873 and 1893, service numbers were allocated on a 'through the door' basis; each man being given a number as he joined the service. Between 1894 and 1907, batches of numbers representing specific branches of the service were used. Therefore, men joining the Seamen and Communication branch were given numbers within a certain range and men joining the Stokers branch were given a number in a different range. All of the service numbers between 1873 and 1907 are in one sequence from 40001 to 366450.

In 1908 a new service numbering system was started with all branches of the services beginning again at 1, but this time the branches of the service were given different alphabetical prefixes to identify them. Therefore men joining from 1908 into the Seamen branch had service numbers prefixed with the letter 'J' and men joining the Stoker branch had service numbers prefixed with the letter 'K'.

With the creation of the Royal Naval Air Service in July 1914, the Royal Navy started a new series of service numbers for ratings joining the new service. This was prefixed with an 'F'. Many men already serving in the Royal Navy transferred into the RNAS and kept their original service numbers and it is therefore possible to find men of the RNAS with both numerical service numbers and service numbers with alphabetical prefixes. The range of indexes available is:

ADM 188 A–Z INDEX
Men serving in 1873 or who
     enlisted between then and 1891   ADM188/245–67
Enlistments, 1892–1912   ADM 188/1132–54
Enlistments, 1913–23   ADM 188/1155–77

ADM 188 RECORDS OF SERVICE (SPECIFICALLY RNAS)
Service numbers F1–F55000   ADM 188/560–646

An alphabetical register of Royal Marines who transferred into the RNAS between May 1912 and September 1917 can be found in ADM 159/212.

6.2.2 *AIR 1*
Although there are numerous files in AIR 1 concerning RNAS officers, there are very few which specifically concern RNAS ratings alone. Most files which mention RNAS ratings are to be found under unit records.

6.2.3 *ADM 116*
Although the records in ADM 116 cover a wide variety of subjects, the series is not primarily concerned with records of service. However, two files about RNAS ratings who were members of the RNAS Armoured Car Section in Russia can be found in ADM 116/1625 and 1717. Details relating to such subjects as individuals' discipline and awards received, not readily available in other files, together with information contained in ADM 188, can be found here.

6.3   Case Study

Family photographs (Fig. 15) can provide lots of useful information about individuals, even if you have only their names. See chapter 14 for further details about photographs.

6.3.1 *Arthur Bedward Spencer*
A.B. Spencer was one of the many young men who answered his country's call for volunteers at the outbreak of the First World War. As the

Fig. 15 *Petty Officer Mechanic A. B. Spencer.*

photograph of A.B. Spencer clearly showed him in the uniform of a Petty Officer of the RNAS Armoured Car Section, the logical place to start was the name index to `ratings in ADM 188. An entry in ADM 188/1174 showed an Arthur B. Spencer with an RNAS service number of F1769. Service number F1769 is to be found in ADM 188/563. See Fig. 16.

Born in Old Basford, Nottingham, on 15 April 1891, Arthur Spencer volunteered for service as a Petty Officer Mechanic in the Royal Naval Air Service on 9 November 1914. His engagement papers (held by the Fleet Air Arm Museum) describe him as 5'11½" tall, with auburn hair, grey eyes and a fresh complexion. His occupation on enlistment was given as hosiery manufacturer.

Further details, contained in ADM 188/563, show that after basic military training Spencer was posted to an RNAS Armoured Car Unit and it was with this unit that he was to see his initial operational service. Although no annotation was made on his ADM 188 record, consultation of the medal roll in ADM 171/115 showed that he qualified for a 1914/15 Star, British War Medal and Victory Medal. However, the 'How Disposed of Column' is blank with a note to 'see officers roll'. This note indicates that at some stage in the war, Spencer was commissioned from the ranks.

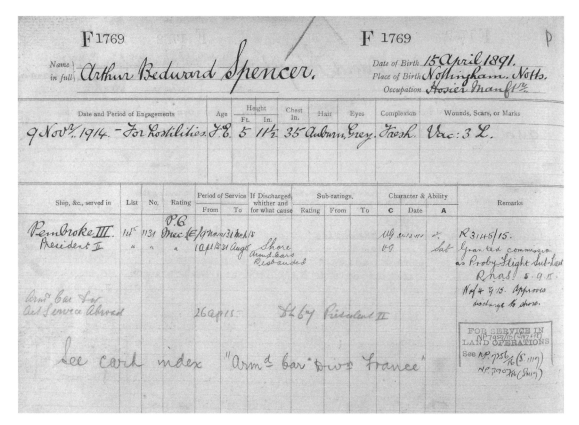

F 1769   F 1769   p

Name in full *Arthur Bedward Spencer.*

Date of Birth *15 April 1891.*
Place of Birth *Nottingham. Notts.*
Occupation *Hosier Manf¹ᵉ*

Date and Period of Engagements	Age	Height Ft. In.	Chest In.	Hair	Eyes	Complexion	Wounds, Scars, or Marks
9 Nov.ʳ 1914. - For Hostilities.	*F.E.*	*5 11½*	*35*	*Auburn.*	*Grey.*	*Fresh.*	*Vac: 3 L.*

Ship, &c., served in	List	No.	Rating	Period of Service From / To	If Discharged, whither and for what cause	Sub-ratings. Rating / From / To	Character & Ability C / Date / A	Remarks
Pembroke III.	14ˢ	1131	*P.6 Mec (E)*	*9 Nov 31 Mch/15*			*VG 31.12.41*	*R 3145/15.*
President II	"	"	"	*1 Apl 15 31 Aug/15 Shore Armd Cars Disbanded*			*VG Sat*	*Granted commission as Proby Flight Sub-Lieut RNAS 5.9.15. N of 4 9/15. Approves discharge to shore.*
Armd Car for Act Service Abroad				*26 Ap 15*	*H by President II*			

See card index "Armd Car Divn France"

FOR SERVICE IN LAND OPERATIONS
See *N.P. 7456/16 (S.1117)*
N.P. 790 /16 (S.117)

Fig. 16 *The Royal Naval Air Service rating's record of service for Arthur Bedward Spencer.* ADM 188/563

Further consultation of his ADM 188 record showed a faint note stating that PO(M) A.B. Spencer was commissioned as a Probationary Flight Sub Lieutenant (FSL) on 5 September 1915. This was confirmed by looking at the *Navy List.*

The records of service of RNAS officers in ADM 273 show three different entries for the trainee pilot: ADM 273/7 ff74, ADM 273/23 ff211 and ADM 273/30 ff133. The first of these three entries notes that he joined the RNAS school at Eastchurch on 20 September 1915, and after a period of instruction was awarded Royal Aero Club Flying Certificate 1903, on 16 October 1915 (see Fig. 17).

After basic flying training, a posting to the RNAS air station at Killingholme with effect from 20 October 1915 for further flying instruction was to result in an unfortunate end to what appeared to have been a promising flying career. Confidential reports in ADM 273/7 dated 20 December 1915 record that Arthur Spencer lost his flying nerve. Although described as 'a good officer so far as he has gone and [has been] one of the best pupils', Spencer's flying days were over.

Royal Navy Aircraft Serials and Units 1911–1919 by Ray Sturtivant and Gordon Page has a very useful index of names of individuals associated with RNAS aircraft. Interestingly, an entry for FSL A.B. Spencer notes that whilst he was flying BE2C, serial number 1137, with Flight Lieutenant J.C. Brook, from Killingholme, the plane nose-dived into the Humber. Considering the date of the accident and the content of the confidential reports in ADM 273/7, it appears that this accident was the most likely cause of Spencer's loss of flying nerve.

Obviously a man of ability, FSL Spencer then spent a short period at sea aboard HMS *Penelope* before taking up a commission in the Royal Naval Volunteer Reserve (RNVR) as an armaments officer, still serving with, rather than in, the RNAS. The RNVR record of service for S/Lt A.B. Spencer RNVR can be found in ADM 337/121 folio 66.

With effect from 24 January 1916, Sub Lieutenant A.B. Spencer RNVR served as an armaments officer at a variety of RNAS air stations. Although technically an officer of the RNVR, Spencer's confidential reports were still completed by RNAS officers. All of the reports state that he was a good officer, hardworking and trustworthy, and recommended for promotion.

Eventually promoted to Lieutenant RNVR, Arthur Spencer was one of the many naval officers connected with aviation who transferred to the fledgling RAF on 1 April 1918. Not surprisingly his name appears in the first *Air Force List* in April 1918. His RAF record of service in AIR 76/477 notes that after continuing his duties at Cattewater in Plymouth until after the armistice, he was eventually placed on the RAF unemployed list and retired from the RAF as Captain in July 1919.

Arthur Bedward Spencer died in 1938.

Fig. 17 *The photograph on Flight Sub Lieutenant A.B. Spencer's Flying certificate.*

7 ROYAL AIR FORCE AND WOMEN'S ROYAL AIR FORCE RECORDS OF SERVICE

Although many of the records of service of RAF personnel were created before the formation of the RAF, in this chapter only records of service created after 31 March 1918 or which were administered by the Air Ministry, i.e. records in the AIR record series, will be discussed.

The formal creation of the RAF on 1 April 1918 established a service which by the armistice had 27,333 officers and 263,837 other ranks. As the manpower for the new service came from the Admiralty and War Office, the Air Ministry had to set about acquiring or creating records relating to the manpower it had just inherited.

7.1 Officers

Records of service concerning RAF officers fall into two generic groups: records of service in one collection and records which contain details relating to officers' services amongst the squadron records in AIR 1. The other key source concerning RAF officers, especially those who saw service after 1919, is the *Air Force List*.

The first *Air Force List* appeared in April 1918 and listed all of those officers who joined the new service upon its creation. Interestingly, the ranks used in the early *Air Force Lists* are both naval and military. RAF ranks as used today did not appear until April 1919.

From April 1920 until March 1939 the *Air Force List* contains quite detailed information about the location and names of officers in given units. *Retired Lists* first appeared in the spring of 1949. The *Retired Lists* provide date of birth, qualifications and honours and awards, date of first commission, date of retirement and the date of the commission of the highest rank attained.

7.1.1 AIR 76

The record series AIR 76, which is available only on microfilm, comprises 567 reels of microfilm containing the records of service of most of the early officers of the RAF. The record series, which is arranged alphabetically,

See instructions for use of this form in K. R. and A. C. I, and notes in R. A. F. Field Service Pocket Book,

OPERATIONS RECORD BOOK

of (Unit or Formation)...... NO. 159 Squadron. R.A.F. ......

Air Force (India) Form 540

No. of pages used for day......................

Place.	Date.	Time.	Summary of Events.	References to Appendices.
			SPORTS NOTES continued....	

Summary of Events:

SPORTS NOTES continued....

Before the move from Digri, hockey was becoming very popular and several games were played. It is hoped to begin a Hockey League. On March 31st a Softball Game between Aircrew Sergeants and Aircrew Officers took place. Although a number of the players had not played the game previously, a very amusing and enjoyable evening resulted. The aircrew sergeants were the winners by 16-15.

MEDICAL NOTES.

On March 7th, No. 159 Squadron moved to Dhubalia. In the main it can be said that the station was far from being ready for the reception of a Heavy Bomber Squadron.

Cookhouses: These were in a gross state of unpreparedness. Washing-up facilities and even cooking arrangements were inadequate. Drainage was primitive and dangerous - dangerous in so much as disposal of sullage favoured fly-breeding with consequent health dangers.

Water Supply: Two water points existed for the whole squadron - one for officers and one for Senior N.C.O.s, N.C.O.s and airmen. These water points consisted of one tap per point. It is unnecessary to comment further.

Malaria: The malaria in this area is high among the natives - it will be high among R.A.F. personnel, because a considerable number of Indians living in the camp area must form a vast reservoir of infection. There is at least one big Indian village between the Domestic and Technical sites. It is needless to add that the health, even the very lives of Squadron personnel will be menaced by malaria and other communicable diseases, if these natives and their habitations are allowed to remain in such close proximity to our personnel.

OFFICERS PROMOTIONS AND POSTINGS.

F/O.E.J.D. Stanley (114064 GD(P)) promoted to F/Lt. (WS) w.e.f 9.12.43.
P/O.B. Clifton DFM. (50589 GD(G)) promoted to F/O.(on probation (WS) w.e.f 19.5.43.
F/O.J.H. Watson (Can.J.7802 GD(N)) promoted F/Lt. (WS) w.e.f. 1.1.43.
F/O.J.R. Gauntlett (106221 GD(P)) promoted F/Lt. (WS) w.e.f. 6.9.43.
P/O.T. Titchmarsh (151668 GD(N)) promoted F/O.(onprobation)(WS) w.e.f.19.9.43.
P/O.F.P.A. Heynert (149322 GD(P)) PROMOTED Flying Officer on prob. (WS) w.e.f. 22.7.43.
P/O.J.H.H. Lentz (149321 GD(P))promoted F/O. on prob. (WS) w.e.f. 22.7.43.
P/O.H.F. Kerley (134741 GD(N)) promoted F/O. on prob. (WS) w.e.f. 3.12.43.
F/O.K.H. Mills (117471 GD(G)) posted from No. 1673 Flight w.e.f. 9.1.44.
(55091 GD(P)) P/O. Barlow posted,ex U.K. w.e.f. 14.2.44.
F/O. Robinson (Aus.426239 GD(P)) posted,ex U.K. 14.2.44.
F/Lt.S.A. Sharpe (45711 GD(P)) posted to No. 1673 H.C.U. w.e.f. 24.2.44.

Fig. 18 *A typical page from a Second World War RAF Squadron Operational Record Book recording postings and non-flying activities.* AIR 27/1061

contains records of service of some 26,000 officers of the RAF whose service ended before the end of 1919. Records of service for officers who served after this date are still held by the Ministry of Defence.

The records in AIR 76 consist of microfilm copies of single-sheet records of service, completed in many cases on both sides, which contain all of the most useful but basic information about an RAF officer. Information in an AIR 76 record includes:

Christian name in full and surname
Date of birth
Permanent home address
Details of next of kin
Units in which an individual served and when
Appointments and promotions (with *London Gazette* dates)
Honours and awards (with *London Gazette* dates)
Medical boards.

Most of the records also note the date on which they were started and in

FAR EAST AIR FORCE

Headquarters—CHANGI.

**Postal Address—HEADQUARTERS, FAR EAST AIR FORCE, CHANGI, SINGAPORE, 17.
Telegraphic Address—PERARDUA, SINGAPORE.*

COMMAND HEADQUARTERS.

Air Marshal Sir FRANCIS FRESSANGES,   Commander-in-Chief 12.11.54
  K.B.E., C.B., i.d.c., p.s.a.

PERSONAL APPOINTMENTS.

Squadron Leader J. D. Thirlwell, D.F.C., p.s.a.   P.S.O. to C.-in-C. 24.1.54
Flight Lieutenant R. G. Price   ..   ..   ..   Aide-de-camp to C.-in-C.   ..   12.11.54

AIR STAFF.

Air Vice-Marshal.
  A. D. Gillmore, C.B., C.B.E., i.d.c.,
    p.s.a. (S.A.S.O.) 17.9.53
Air Plans.
  Group Captain.
    C. Broughton, C.B.E., i.d.c.,
      p.s.a., c.f.s   ..   ..   -.10.55
  Wing Commanders.
    C. N. Foxley-Norris, O.B.E.,
      D.S.O., p.s.a. 15.7.53
    D. H. Sutton, p.s.a.   ..   29.6.55
Operations and Training.
  Group Captain.
    M. H. Rhys, A.F.C., p.s.a., c.f.s.*   17.11.53
  Wing Commanders.
    R. F. Watson, A.F.C., (R.N.Z.A.F.)   19.8.55
    J. G. Topham, D.S.O., O.B.E.,
      D.F.C., p.s.a 2.8.53
    R. J. Sage, A.F.C. 8.10.54
  Squadron Leaders.
    D. W. Barber, p.s.a.   ..   14.6.53
    D. S. Dickens, A.F.C. 23.7.53
    B. L. Duckenfield, A.F.C.   ..   18.2.55
Navigation.
  Wing Commander.
    H. Mansell, p.s.a. 20.6.55
Intelligence.
  Group Captain.
    E. L. J. Rowe, O.B.E.   ..   10.4.54
  Wing Commander.
    E. C. Badcoe, D.F.C. 18.2.55
  Squadron Leaders.
    H. T. Sutton, O.B.E., D.F.C.,
      p.s.a. 7.7.54
    E. A. Jee 30.6.54
    A. C. L. Mackie, D.F.C., p.s.a.,
      c.f.s.* 7.1.54
    A. C. Philip 6.5.54
    W. N. H. Brawn, D.F.C., A.F.C.,
      c.f.s.* 14.8.53
Air Traffic Control.
  Squadron Leader.
    H. Jacobs, D.F.C., A.F.C.   ..   24.10.53
Fighter Control.
  Squadron Leader.
    A. Y. Mason, A.F.C.   ..   15.7.54
Ground Defence.
  Group Captain.
    A. A. Baxter, O.B.E. (S.G.D.S.O.)   21.7.54
  Squadron Leader.
    R. G. M. Hubbard   ..   28.8.55
Signals.
  Group Captain.
    J. A. Robinson, O.B.E., B.A.,
      B.A.I., p.s.a. 20.2.55
  Wing Commander.
    R. G. Burnett, M.B.E. ..   29.10.54
  Squadron Leaders.
    C. O. Cook 7.1.54
    K. Hellawell 28.4.54

STAFFS OF THE SERVICES.
(AIR STAFF)

Photography.
  Squadron Leader.
    C. T. Lynas 4.4.55
Physical Training.
  Squadron Leader.
    G. A. Podevin 23.6.53
Meteorological.
  L. S. Clarkson, M.Sc.   ..   25.3.52
Research.
  J. W. Watts, B.Sc.   ..   ..   —

MISCELLANEOUS ESTABLISHMENT.

H.Q., F.E.A.F. Representative of
  Joint Planning Staff.
  Wing Commander.
    R. A. L. Morant, O.B.E., p.s.a.   30.8.53
  Squadron Leader.
    L. G. Holmes, D.F.C., A.F.C. ..   14.1.55

ADMINISTRATIVE STAFF.

Air Vice-Marshal.
  E. C. Bates, C.B.E., A.F.C., i.d.c.,
    c.f.s.* 1.11.55
Organisation.
  Group Captain.
    H. E. Hopkins, D.F.C., A.F.C.,
      j.s.s.c., q.s., c.f.s.*   ..   10.7.55
  Wing Commanders.
    H. A. Lax, p.s.a.   ..   27.1.53
    N. E. Hext, M.B.E.   ..   16.6.53
    A. S. Mann, D.F.C., p.s.a.   ..   25.2.54
  Squadron Leader.
    R. C. Everson, A.F.C. ..   20.10.54
Administrative Plans.
  Wing Commander.
    C. S. G. Stanbury, D.S.O.,
      D.F.C., A.F.C., p.s.a., p.f.c., c.f.s.   2.5.54
  Squadron Leader.
    K. H. Bayley, D.F.C., p.s.a. ..   15.8.54
Personnel.
  Group Captain.
    O. A. Morris, D.S.O. (S.P.S.O.)   12.6.53
  Wing Commanders.
    E. H. Lynch-Blosse, O.B.E., p.s.a.,
      c.f.s. 12.5.54
    E. M. Webb 18.2.55
  Squadron Leaders.
    J. R. Robinson, A.F.C.   ..   17.5.55
    R. Brice 11.8.55
    J. A. Henshaw 14.8.55
    N. Wilson, O.B.E.   ..   23.12.54
Personnel (Civilian).
  L. D. Millo (C.Ad.O.)   ..   10.6.51
Airfield Construction.
  Squadron Leader.
    A. R. Young 10.12.54

*Official correspondence should be addressed to : Overseas Registry, Whitehall, London, S.W.1.

Fig. 19 *A post-war
Confidential Air Force
List January 1956.*
AIR 10/7371

which unit an individual was commissioned, if not directly into the RFC or RAF.

It is interesting to note that AIR 76 contains records of service of many RFC officers who lost their lives prior to the formation of the RAF.

7.1.2   *AIR 1*

There are numerous files in AIR 1 which contain details relating to RAF officers, both general files and files specific to given units. The wide variety of files includes many which cover both the RFC period and the RAF period from 1 April 1918 onwards. Included are files on:

> Officers' flying times
> Appointments and postings
> Nominal rolls
> Lists of prisoners of war
> Dispositions of officers

Of these files some relate to officers who, of course, stayed in the RAF after 1919 and for whom there is no record in AIR 76. Some of the most important of these files include:

> Nominal roll of officers recommended for
>   permanent commissions: RAF, May–August 1918   AIR 1/1161/204/5/2516
> Nominal roll of officers recommended for permanent
>   commissions: RAF, August–September 1919   AIR 1/1161/204/5/2517
> Nominal roll of officers granted permanent commissions:
>   RAF, August–September 1919   AIR 1/1161/204/5/2518
> Permanent commissions for officers seconded from
>   the Army to the RAF, August–September 1919   AIR 1/1161/204/5/2520
> Nominal rolls of officers who refused or accepted
>   RAF commissions, August–September 1919   AIR 1/1161/204/5/2521

Other files of note include:

> Nominal roll of South African officers serving with the RAF,
>   December 1918   AIR 1/2418/305/7
> Reports on Canadian officers with the RAF, in the field,
>   June–December 1918   AIR 1/1035/204/5/1452

The First World War and post-First World War flying and war/service experiences of some RAF officers who went to the RAF Staff College after 1918 and who wrote up their experiences as part of their college course, can be found in AIR 1/2386/228/11/1 to AIR 1/2392/228/22/188. These essays can be searched for by name and include many of the most significant and senior RAF commanders of the period, starting with Charles Portal.

7.2 Airmen

There are a number of different sources where details about RAF airmen can be found, in collections of service papers in one record series (AIR 79), as well as details distributed amongst the squadron records in AIR 1. The single most important source concerning RAF other ranks, on formation of the service, is the RAF muster. This muster lists by service number all of those men who were on the strength of the new service when it was formed. Beyond name and service number, the muster gives date of enlistment into the services, trade, period of engagement and rate of pay. The RAF muster can be found in AIR 1/819/204/4/1316.

7.2.1 AIR 79

To search these records you need to know the service number of the individual you seek (see 7.2.2).

The service records of RAF airmen with service numbers up to 329 000 are in the record series AIR 79. This record series is arranged in service number order. Although it contains the records of men whose service numbers go up to 329 000, the records of many men whose service numbers lie within this range but who saw service in the Second World War are not in this record series but are retained by the Ministry of Defence.

As AIR 79 contains records up to service number 329000, it therefore holds the records of men who formerly served in the RE Balloon Section, the Royal Flying Corps, the Royal Naval Air Service and those who entered directly into the RAF. The records are arranged as follows:

References	Service numbers
AIR 79/1–2805	RAF service numbers 1–329000
AIR 79/2806	South African Air Corps service numbers Z2–Z592
AIR 79/2807	RAF Special Reservist service numbers SR1–SR25

As each piece of AIR 79 only covers a given range of service numbers it is necessary to obtain the correct service number from AIR 78, if it is not known already.

Although the RAF service numbers are in a logical numerical sequence, they do not necessarily represent a chronological sequence of enlistments. The lowest numbers represent those men who joined the RFC on formation, and the highest those men who joined the RAF in the immediate post-First World War period. Service numbers between 200001 and 255600 represent former members of the RNAS with RN service numbers F1–F55600. Service numbers 313000–315000 represent men who originally joined the Royal Navy prior to July 1914 and who subsequently joined the RNAS but retained their original RN service numbers until they joined the RAF.

Fig. 20 (facing) *Confidential Air Force List May 1944.* AIR 10/3834

No. 100 GROUP.

(BOMBER COMMAND.)

Postal Address—" BYLAUGH HALL", EAST DEREHAM, NORFOLK.

Telegraphic Address—AIRGROUP, DEREHAM.

Telephone No.—DEREHAM 312.

R.A.F. Station .. .. .. Foulsham.	R.A.F. Station .. .. .. Sculthorpe.
No. 192 Squadron.	No. 214 Squadron.
R.A.F. Station .. .. .. Great	R.A.F. Station .. .. .. Swannington.
Massingham.	
R.A.F. Station .. .. .. Little Snoring.	R.A.F. Station .. .. .. West
No. 169 Squadron.	Servicing Section. Raynham.
No. 515 Squadron.	S.D. Development Unit.
No. 1692 Flight.	No. 141 Squadron.
Satellites .. .. Oulton.	No. 239 Squadron.
North Creake.	No. 1694 Flight.
R.A.F. Station .. .. .. Radlett.	Communication Flight .. .. Swanton
No. 80 (Sig.) Wing.	Morley.

Air Cdre. E. B. ADDISON, *C.B.E., p.s.a.*	*Air Officer Commanding*	8Nov.43

AIR STAFF.

Gp. Capt. R. A. Chisholm, *D.S.O., D.F.C.*............	*S.A.S.O.*.....................	3Dec43
Wg. Cdr. D. W. Donaldson, *D.S.O., D.F.C.*.........	....	15Dec.43
Wg. Cdr. W. K. Davison, *D.F.C.*...................	....	29Dec.43
Wg. Cdr. L. W. Wells, *O.B.E.*....................	....	13Dec.43
Wg. Cdr. C. V. Winn, *D.F.C.*....................	....	13Dec.43
Sqn. Ldr. E. A. Latter...................	....	6Dec.43
Sqn. Ldr. A. E. Foster...................	....	8Dec.43
Sqn. Ldr. C. E. Knowles, *D.F.C.*............	....	2Feb.44
Sqn. Ldr. N. R. G. Hunter..............	....	14Mar.44
Sqn. Ldr. H. B. Martin, *D.S.O., D.F.C.*	....	21Mar.44

ADMINISTRATIVE STAFF.

Wg. Cdr. E. K. Porte, *O.B.E.*....................	*S.O.A.*....................	27Nov.43
Sqn. Ldr. J. F. B. Ewen...................	*Org.*....................	6Dec.43
Sqn. Ldr. A. A. C. Bellinger...................	*S.P.S.O.*....................	6Dec.43

STAFFS OF THE SERVICES.

Navigation.		
Sqn. Ldr. E. L. Ifould, *D.S.O., D.F.C.*.........	....	2Jan.44
Engineer.		
Wg. Cdr. R. L. Bloodworth...................		30Dec.43
Sqn. Ldr. H. D. Phillips...................		20Dec.43
Signals.		
Gp. Capt. N. G. Goodman...................		10Jan.44
Sqn. Ldr. N. C. Cordingley, *M.B.E.*................		18Dec.43
Sqn. Ldr. H. C. Taylor...................		6Dec.43
Sqn. Ldr. W. McMenemy...................		2Feb.44
Sqn. Ldr. F. P. Smith...................		28Dec.43
Armament.		
Sqn. Ldr. H. J. Bignell...................		13Dec.43
Equipment.		
Sqn. Ldr. A. Leeming...................		6Dec.43
Medical.		
Wg. Cdr. R. E. W. Fisher, *M.B., B.Ch.*........		6Dec.43
Educational.		
*B. M. A. Folland, *M.A.*...................		8Apr.44
Meteorological.		
R. Frost, *B.A.*...................		—

W.A.A.F. STAFF OFFICER.

Sqn. Off. M. W. W. Ford...................		31Dec.43

R.A.F. REGIMENT.

		24Jan.44

As the service origin of men whose records can be found in AIR 79 includes all three services, so a physical variety of the different types of records, all containing similar sorts of information, may be found. Army Forms for men of the RE Balloon and RAF Forms 175 are common examples of what may be found. The RAF used examples of both Naval and Army forms to keep records on their personnel.

Details found in AIR 79 include the usual physical description, date and place of birth data, together with enlistment and discharge dates. Depending on the type of record held in AIR 79 the type and amount of information may then vary. In most cases if a man joined the RAF from the RNAS or Army, then the relevant dates will be annotated on his RAF record. Most RAF records are on an RAF Form 175 and as such contain the following details:

Date and place of birth
Physical description
Dates of attestation and discharge
Cause of discharge
Dates of promotions
Postings
Details of next of kin (wife and children as applicable)
Medical and disciplinary history
Details of medals.

7.2.2 AIR 78

A nominal index of both RAF airmen and WRAF women is available on microfilm in the Open Reading Room. The index, which is of variable quality, provides the surname and first name or initial(s) and the service number, which you need to use AIR 79. Once you have the service number of the airman you seek, apply that number to the AIR 79 series list and order the piece of AIR 79 which encompasses that service number. (For women, see below.) There is an important caveat when using the AIR 78 index. The index covers airmen and airwomen who joined the RAF between 1918 and 1975 and it therefore lists many individuals for whom the National Archives have yet to receive records of service. In the context of current holdings in AIR 79, any number found in AIR 78 must be lower than 329001. Service records with numbers higher than 329000 are still held by the RAF.

7.2.3 AIR 1

There are numerous files within AIR 1 which contain details about RAF airmen, but once again they are dispersed amongst the various units' records, rather than in a specific section. If you know a unit in which an individual served, try a keyword search on the Catalogue.

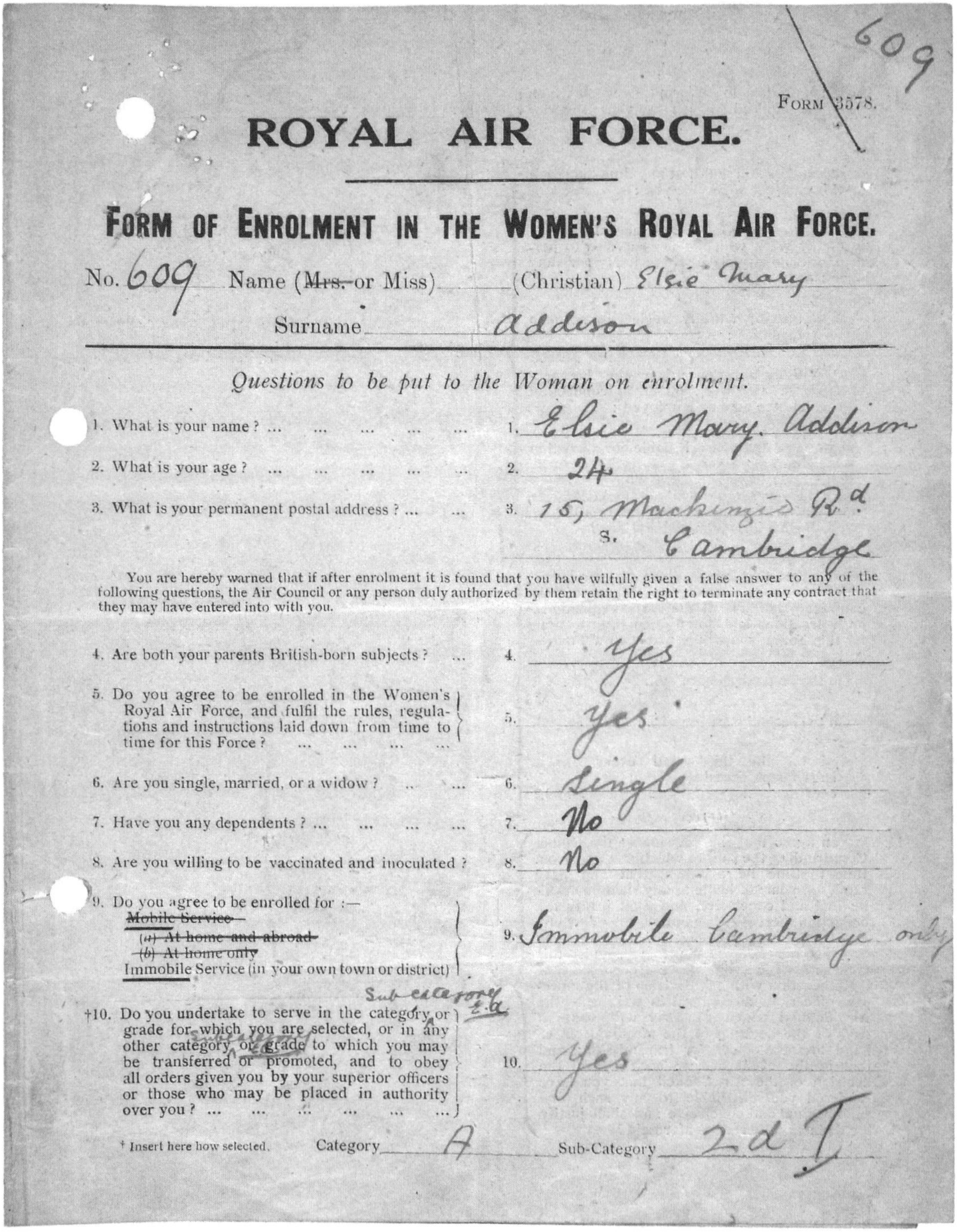

ROYAL AIR FORCE.

FORM OF ENROLMENT IN THE WOMEN'S ROYAL AIR FORCE.

No. *609* Name (Mrs. or Miss) .... (Christian) *Elsie Mary*

Surname .... *Addison*

Questions to be put to the Woman on enrolment.

1. What is your name? ... ... 1. *Elsie Mary. Addison*

2. What is your age? 2. *24*

3. What is your permanent postal address? ... 3. *15, Mackenzie Rd.*
   s. *Cambridge*

You are hereby warned that if after enrolment it is found that you have wilfully given a false answer to any of the following questions, the Air Council or any person duly authorized by them retain the right to terminate any contract that they may have entered into with you.

4. Are both your parents British-born subjects? ... 4. *Yes*

5. Do you agree to be enrolled in the Women's Royal Air Force, and fulfil the rules, regulations and instructions laid down from time to time for this Force? ... ... 5. *Yes*

6. Are you single, married, or a widow? ... ... 6. *Single*

7. Have you any dependents? ... ... 7. *No*

8. Are you willing to be vaccinated and inoculated? 8. *No*

9. Do you agree to be enrolled for :—
   ~~Mobile Service~~
   ~~(a) At home and abroad~~
   ~~(b) At home only~~
   Immobile Service (in your own town or district) 9. *Immobile Cambridge only*

Sub category E.a

†10. Do you undertake to serve in the category or grade for which you are selected, or in any other category or grade to which you may be transferred or promoted, and to obey all orders given you by your superior officers or those who may be placed in authority over you? ... ... 10. *Yes*

† Insert here how selected.   Category *A*   Sub-Category *2d I*

Fig. 22 *WRAF record of service.* AIR 80/2

7.3   Women's Royal Air Force

No records of service of officers of the WRAF have survived.

The surviving records of service of other rank members of the WRAF are in the record series AIR 80. These records have been digitized and placed on DocumentsOnline, where it is possible to search by name.

The original records in this series are arranged alphabetically and therefore no service number is needed to search them. In most cases there is only a single record sheet giving details about each woman. These record sheets vary, and with them the type and amount of information given about each individual. They all give a physical description of the individuals concerned, and details of how and where they were employed. The most unusual terms to be found on these records of service are 'Mobile' and 'Immobile'. Mobile members of the WRAF were full-time members of the service who lived on the camp where they worked or in lodgings nearby, and who were therefore able to be posted anywhere. Immobile members of the WRAF were part-time staff who lived at home.

The records of service are usually found on either Army Form B103 or RAF Form 3677 Z, both of which contain details of length of service and trade. An example of an AIR 80 record can be seen in Fig. 22.

7.4   Special Operations Executive

The records of service of the Special Operations Executive (SOE) can be found in the series HS 9. A number of SOE agents were transferred into SOE from the RAF, whilst others were granted temporary commissions in the Royal Air Force Volunteer Reserve (RAFVR).

The records in HS 9 are arranged in alphabetical order and as such can be searched for by name on the Catalogue.

Amongst those members of SOE who were granted commissions in the RAFVR was Forest Frederick Edward Yeo-Thomas, also known as the 'White Rabbit'.

7.5   Case Study

7.5.1   *Ernest Albert Hogg*
Ernest Albert Hogg initially volunteered to serve in the Army, under the 'Derby Scheme', in December 1915. His chosen regiment was 20 Battalion, King's Royal Rifle Corps. When he was called up for service in May 1916, instead of joining his chosen regiment, he opted to transfer into the Royal Flying Corps.

On mobilization, Hogg, allocated the RFC service number 103993, was described as 5′7″ tall, with dark hair, blue eyes and a fresh complexion. Born in Bermondsey, south London, on 16 September 1894, Ernest Hogg was to spend the next four years at various RFC and latterly RAF units, in both the United Kingdom and France. As he had been an electrical fitter in civilian life, it was not surprising to find him graded as an Air Fitter shortly after some basic RFC training.

Hogg's first operational service overseas was with No.2 Aircraft Depot in France between 23 August and 3 September 1917. A short introduction to active service was ended when he became ill with, as far as his record is concerned, an unknown ailment.

Returning to France in February 1918, Hogg was to serve there until September 1919. Finally being demobilized in April 1920, it appears that Hogg resumed his pre-war trade. However, with the emerging German threat of the late 1930s, he joined the RAF Reserve on 17 July 1939. What became of him after that date is at present unknown.

Ernest Hogg's record of service can be found in AIR 79/936.

Fig. 23 *A typical page from a normal Air Force List May 1944.* AFL

GENERAL DUTIES BRANCH—SQUADRON LEADERS

583		584		585	
Ricketts, H. H. (t)	1July	Ralston, J. R. G., D.S.O., D.F.M. § (w)	1Sept	Harries, R. H., D.S.O., D.F.C. (w)	19Nov
Aldridge, K. A., D.F.C. † (t)	1July	Harvey, N. B. § (w)	7Sept	Middleton, R., A.F.C. § (w)	23Nov
Lydall, J. E. † (t)	1July	Kennedy, J. S., D.F.C. (w)	10Sept	Dinsdale, J. S., D.F.C. † (w)	30Nov
Rook, M., D.F.C. ¶ (t)	1July	Shaw, M. J. A. † (w)	11Sept	Gardiner, W. G., D.F.C., A.F.C. § (w)	1Dec
Hill, M. R. (t)	1July	Haine, R. C., D.F.C. § (w)	11Sept	Samson, A. J., D.F.C. (w)	1Dec
Pain, E. M., D.F.C. (t)	1July	Park, G. R., D.F.C. (w)	18Sept	Crowley-Milling, D., D.S.O., D.F.C. (w)	4Dec
Irving, E. H., A.F.C. (t)	1July	Coe, O. D. B., D.F.C. (2nd Lt., Cheshire R. (T.A.) § (w)	26Sept	Langton, R. T., D.F.M. § (w)	7Dec
Robson, N. C. H. † (t)	1July	Macpherson, W. D. (w)	28Sept	A. Reynolds, P. J. B., O.B.E.(w)	8Dec
Lindsay, D. S., D.F.C. † (t)	1July	Secretan, D., D.F.C. † (w)	28Sept	Duke-Woolley, H. B. (w)	8Dec
N.Baker, E. R., D.F.C. † (t)	1July	Coles, W. E., D.F.C., A.F.C. † (w)	30Sept	Dobson, P., D.F.C. (w)	8Dec
Stewart, C. L. W., A.F.C. † (t)	1July	Everitt, G. H., D.S.O., D.F.C. (w)	10Oct	Somerville, K.J., D.F.C., A.F.C. † (w)	18Dec
Kendal, S. R. † (t)	1July	Linney, A. S., O.B.E. † (w)	4Oct	Cracknell, D. A., D.F.C. (w)	24Dec
Cooper, C. C. F. † (t)	1July	Gascoyne-Cecil, R. A. V., D.F.C., w.s.(w)	4Oct	Simpson, P. J., D.F.C. † (w)	28Dec
Cassidy, E., D.F.C. † (t)	1July	McDowall, A., D.F.M. (w)	5Oct	**1944**	
Fitzpatrick, D. B. † (t)	1July	Green, C. L., D.F.C. † (w)	7Oct	Drew, G. † (t)	1Jan
Baker, C. C. M. † (t)	1July	Lucas, P. B., D.S.O. D.F.C. (w)	10Oct	Powell, H. P., A.F.C. † (t)	1Jan
Ensor, J. B., D.F.C. † (t)	1July	Lee-Evans, J. A., D.F.C. (w)	11Oct	Morrison, T. R. (t)	1Jan
Acworth, R. A., D.F.C. † (t)	1July	Bary, R. E., D.F.C. † (w)	16Oct	Powell, G. F., D.F.C. (w)	1Jan
Norris, S. C., D.F.C. † (t)	1July	Crawoford-Compton, W. V., D.S.O., D.F.C. (w)	20Oct	Ashby, E. J. (t)	1Jan
Morley-Mower, G. F., D.F.C.	1July	Davies, D. E., D.F.C., A.F.C. (w)	21Oct	Cruickshank, H. L. (t)	1Jan
Woodman, D. M. † (t)	1July	Lawson, H. R., D.F.C., A.F.C. § (w)	21Oct	Wood, J. D. (t)	1Jan
Jones, L. L., D.F.C., A.F.C. † (t)	1July	Alldis, C. A., D.F.C.(w)	29Oct	Monk, C. L. (q.s. war) † (t)	1Jan
Powell, C. E. L., q.s. (w) † (w. 5 July 43) (t)	1July	Ritchie, W. W. T., A.F.C. † (w)	31Oct	Helsby, R. R. † (t)	1Jan
Winn, C. V., D.F.C. † (t)	1July	Deacon, E. W., D.S.O., D.F.C. § (w)	31Oct	Cragg, F. T. (t)	1Jan
Gordon, P. S., w.s. § (t)	1July	Grant, G. F., D.S.O., D.F.C. § (w)	1Nov	Forster, H. J. ‡ (t)	1Jan
McIntosh, D., D.F.C. § (w)	12July	Eliot, H. W., D.F.C. § (w)	1Nov	Aitkens, I. L. B. § (t)	1Jan
Hallows, B. R. W., D.F.C. (w)	12July	Forbes, J. D. R. § (w)	1Nov	Brandt, J., D.F.C. † (t)	1Jan
Oliver, P., D.F.C. (w)	17July	Cooke, J. K. M., D.S.O., D.F.C. † (w)	3Nov	Haggar, S. P. (t)	1Jan
Wilkerson, D. S. S., D.F.C. (w)	20July	Bradshaw, W., D.F.C. § (w)	5Nov	Adderley, M. C., A.F.C. † (t)	1Jan
Dean, D. F. E. C., D.S.O., D.F.C. (Lt. R.A. (T.A.) (w)	22July	Pierce, T. R. † (w)	8Nov	Dendy, J. ‡ (t)	1Jan
Selby, J. B., D.S.O. D.F.C. (w)	25July	Charles, E. F. J., D.S.O., D.F.C. § (w)	9Nov	Alderton, A. M. L. † (t)	1Jan
Llewellyn, T. H. A., A.F.C. (w)	1Aug	Yule, R. D., D.S.O., D.F.C. § (w)	9Nov	Davies, L. W. † (t)	1Jan
Dunkerley, C. § (w)	1Aug	Dart, A. P. ... D.S.O.		Ruffell, A. W. ‡ (t)	1Jan
Perfect, W. T. (w)	3Aug			Cumberland, W. P. † (t)	1Jan
Le Cheminant, P. de L., D.F.C. § (w)	4Aug			I. Waymouth, T. G. †.(t)	1Jan
				Tasker, N. † (t)	1Jan
				N. Clift, J., O.B.E. † (t)	1Jan
				Harris, R. L. H. † (t)	1Jan
				Law, R. C. E. (t)	1Jan
				McLaren, A. D., D.F.C. † (t)	1Jan
				Peck, B. E., D.F.C. † (t)	1Jan
				Jordan, J. E. † (t)	1Jan

8 OPERATIONAL RECORDS

The term 'operations' suggests activities against an enemy, be they in the air or on the ground. Operations against an enemy may be further defined as 'active operations'. However, the nature of flying operations in peace or war is such that detailed records are created showing the planning, execution and aftermath of such operations.

A fighter patrol in the First World War, a bombing raid in the Second World War and a helicopter-borne search and rescue mission could all be free of incident apart from the basic execution of the task. The amount of paperwork created around such operations could be as brief as a one-line entry in an operational record book. On other occasions the amount of paperwork (and therefore the archival trail) may be so great that it could take weeks or even years to look at all of the papers.

The challenges for researchers of aviation operations are plenty. Apart from wanting to know who took part, where and when, they also need to know what is available, how it is described and how to access it. The following sections will cover some of the basic records and significant events in aviation history. With the advent of the Catalogue, it is much easier to search the records of the National Archives, but certain knowledge and understanding of the RFC, RNAS, RAF, FAA and AAC always helps.

Locating operational records amongst the ADM, AIR, DEFE and WO records is much easier than it was 10 years ago. Keyword searching the Catalogue can help. Using such search terms as the unit involved or the place will provide plenty of results. Combined word searches using 'operation' AND the place will make searches more effective.

8.1 Royal Engineers Balloon Section

As there were so few military operations in which the Royal Engineers Balloon Sections were involved, the records relating to these operations are few.

A general report relating to balloons, covering the period 1885–6, which covers the first major use of balloons in Bechuanaland and the

Sudan, can be found in WO 32/6067 (Code 45(N)). A report from the Officer Commanding Royal Engineers in Bechuanaland in 1885 can be found in WO 32/8204 (Code O(AU)). Further reports relating to British Army operations in the same region can be found in WO 33/44 (see Fig. 3) and 45, WO 106/264, 6242 and 6243 and WO 147/29 and 35.

Nos.1–3 Balloon Sections, Royal Engineers, were involved in the Boer War. A summary of the role of the Royal Engineers in the Boer War can be found in WO 108/283–298.

A report of the employment of No.4 Balloon Section, Royal Engineers in China, 1900–2, can be found in WO 32/6059 (Code O(J)).

8.2   Royal Flying Corps

Operational records for brigades, wings, squadrons and miscellaneous units of the Royal Flying Corps can be found in AIR 1. Whether the unit is a brigade, wing or squadron, as long as the number or name of that unit is known, then the operational records of that unit can be found.

Many different types of operational records exist in AIR 1, not only squadron record books and summaries of work but also reports of activities, combat reports, hours flown, particulars of officers and numerous photographs.

Most of the operational records contain such data as what the task was, who was involved, when the operation took place and what the outcome was. To create a full picture of a particular operation or incident it may be necessary to consult a number of sources. By using operational records from each part of the chain of command, from the unit the man was serving in at the time upwards, a more informative account of a given incident can be created.

Beyond the records in AIR 1, it is also possible to find general reports of RFC activities in WO 158.

Records of a number of squadrons are also in AIR 1. These records can be found by using the squadron number as the keyword when searching the 'Online Lists'. They usually provide overall statistics concerning unit performance, awards and kills, together with a brief history of the unit. These histories can also be found by using the unit index in the AIR 1 class list.

A typical example of an RFC squadron operational record, in this case a 16 Squadron, RFC, Work Summary (AIR 1/1253/204/8/9), can be seen in Fig. 14.

8.3 Royal Naval Air Service

Although the RNAS was the responsibility of the Admiralty prior to the formation of the RAF in April 1918, the majority of operational records concerning RNAS squadrons are in AIR 1. As with the RFC squadron records, as long as the number of the squadron is known, the records can easily be found in AIR 1.

The majority of Admiralty records concerning RNAS activities can be found in ADM 137. There are two ways of identifying records in this series. One is to use the ADM 137 lists to identify relevant Admiralty Historical Section records in the record series. The other is to use the Admiralty Index and Digest in ADM 12 to identify original Admiralty file references and then convert them into ADM 137 file references. Beyond using the ADM 12 alphabetical sections to obtain references concerning awards granted to individuals, Digest (Subject) codes 3 (Actions with The Enemy) and 90 (Aviation) will provide the most useful items. Original files referred to in ADM 12 may be found in ADM 1, ADM 116 and ADM 137.

A guide, 'How to Use ADM 12', is available upon request from the Open Reading Room desk.

Operational records of a number of RNAS airship units based in the west of England can be found in the Plymouth Station records in ADM 131/64.

8.4 Royal Air Force: First World War

The creation of the RAF in April 1918 saw a number of changes made to the titles of units that had formerly been part of the RNAS. Since the changes made upon creation of the RAF, further evolutionary changes have occurred during the history of the RAF and these will be noted in the relevant sections.

The RAF operational records for the First World War are in AIR 1, together with those of the RFC and RNAS. The most important item to note when looking for squadron records after April 1918 is that former RNAS squadrons were renumbered into the 200 numerical range. Therefore, 1 Squadron RNAS became 210 Squadron RAF.

Accounts of the experiences of a number of RFC/RAF officers who attended the RAF Staff College after the First World War can be found in AIR 1.

Locations of RFC/RAF between February 1917 and September 1918 are listed in AIR 1/2112/207/52.

Fig. 24 *RFC/RAF Order of Battle, showing which units served in which higher units and how they were structured.*
AIR 1/2129/207/83/1

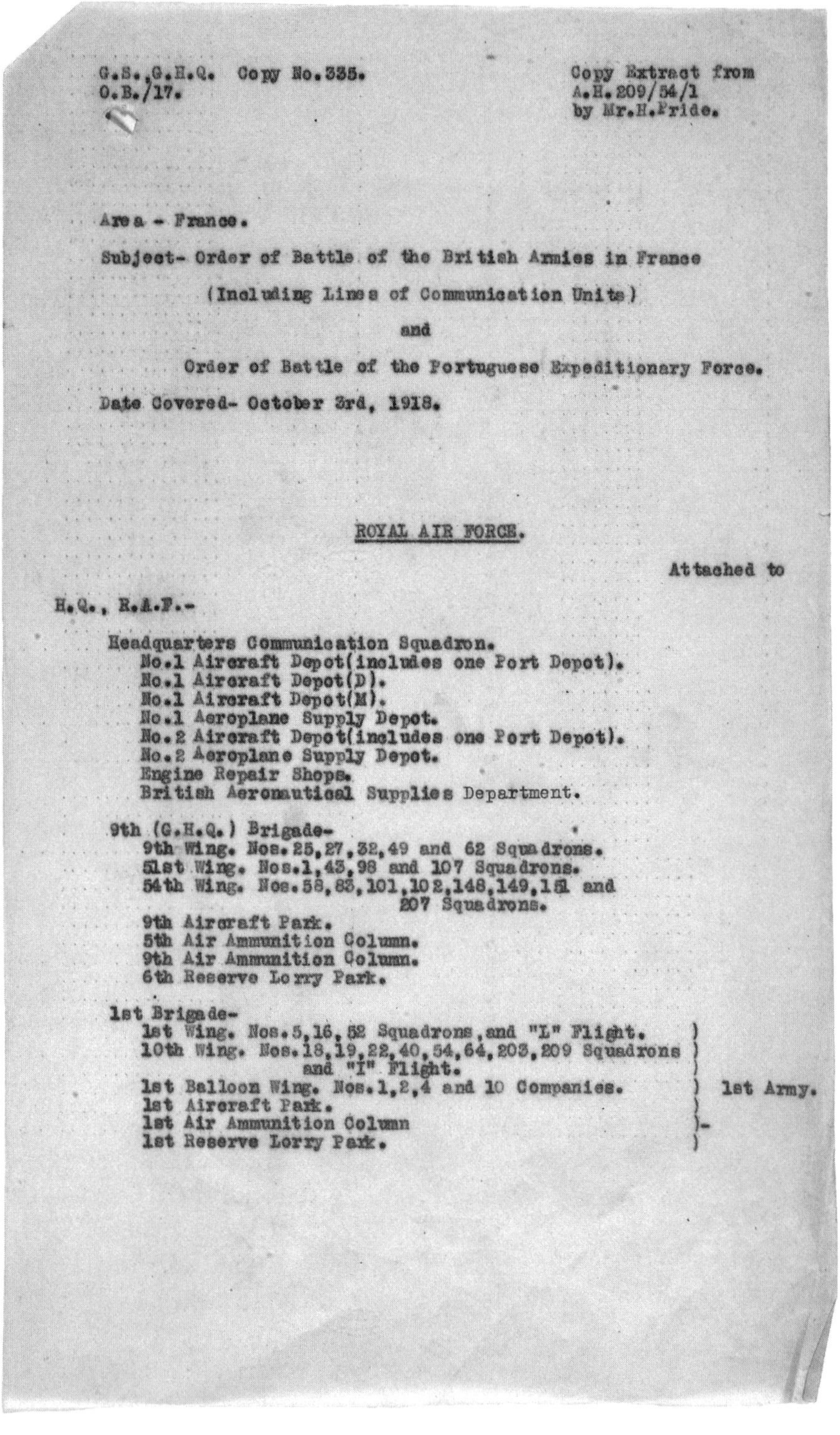

G.S.,G.H.Q.   Copy No.335.   Copy Extract from
O.B./17.   A.H.209/54/1
                                               by Mr.H.Pride.

Area - France.

Subject- Order of Battle of the British Armies in France

    (Including Lines of Communication Units)

    and

    Order of Battle of the Portuguese Expeditionary Force.

Date Covered- October 3rd, 1918.

          ROYAL AIR FORCE.

                                Attached to

H.Q., R.A.F.-

    Headquarters Communication Squadron.
      No.1 Aircraft Depot(includes one Port Depot).
      No.1 Aircraft Depot(D).
      No.1 Aircraft Depot(M).
      No.1 Aeroplane Supply Depot.
      No.2 Aircraft Depot(includes one Port Depot).
      No.2 Aeroplane Supply Depot.
      Engine Repair Shops.
      British Aeronautical Supplies Department.

    9th (G.H.Q.) Brigade-
      9th Wing. Nos.25,27,32,49 and 62 Squadrons.
      51st Wing. Nos.1,43,98 and 107 Squadrons.
      54th Wing. Nos.58,83,101,102,148,149,151 and
                      207 Squadrons.

      9th Aircraft Park.
      5th Air Ammunition Column.
      9th Air Ammunition Column.
      6th Reserve Lorry Park.

    1st Brigade-
      1st Wing. Nos.5,16,52 Squadrons,and "L" Flight.   )
      10th Wing. Nos.18,19,22,40,54,64,203,209 Squadrons)
             and "I" Flight.   )
      1st Balloon Wing. Nos.1,2,4 and 10 Companies.   ) 1st Army.
      1st Aircraft Park.   )
      1st Air Ammunition Column   )-
      1st Reserve Lorry Park.   )

3.

INDEX TO UNITS.

ROYAL AIR FORCE

Unit.	Army.	Unit.	Army.
1st Wing	1st	No.64 Squadron	1st
2nd Wing	2nd	No.65 Squadron	4th
9th Wing	H.Q.	No.70 Squadron	3rd
10th Wing	1st	No.73 Squadron	H.Q.
11th Wing	2nd	No.74 Squadron	2nd
12th Wing	3rd	No.79 Squadron	2nd
13th Wing	3rd	No.80 Squadron	H.Q.
15th Wing	4th	No.82 Squadron	4th
22nd Wing	4th	No.83 Squadron	H.Q.
41st Wing	Ind.Force.	No.84 Squadron	4th
51st Wing	H.Q.	No.85 Squadron	2nd
54th Wing	H.Q.	No.87 Squadron	3rd
65th Wing	5th	No.88 Squadron	5th
80th Wing	5th	No.92 Squadron	5th
81st Wing	5th	No.98 Squadron	H.Q.
No.1 Squadron	2nd	No.99 Squadron	Ind.Force
No.2 Squadron	1st	No.100 Squadron	Ind.Force
No.3 Squadron	3rd	No.101 Squadron	H.Q.
No.4 Squadron	2nd	No.102 Squadron	H.Q.
No.5 Squadron	1st	No.103 Squadron	5th
No.6 Squadron	G.H.Q	No.104 Squadron	Ind.Force
No.7 Squadron	2nd	No.107 Squadron	H.Q.
No.8 Squadron	4th	No.148 Squadron	H.Q.
No.9 Squadron	4th	No.149 Squadron	H.Q.
No.10 Squadron	2nd	No.151 Squadron	H.Q.
No.11 Squadron	3rd	No.201 Squadron	3rd
No.12 Squadron	3rd	No.203 Squadron	1st
No.13 Squadron	1st	No.205 Squadron	4th
No.15 Squadron	3rd	No.206 Squadron	2nd
No.16 Squadron	1st	No.207 Squadron	H.Q.
No.18 Squadron	1st	No.208 Squadron	1st
No.19 Squadron	1st	No.209 Squadron	4th
No.20 Squadron	2nd	No.210 Squadron	2nd
No.21 Squadron	5th	No.211 Squadron	5th
No.22 Squadron	1st	No.215 Squadron	H.Q.
No.23 Squadron	4th	No.216 Squadron	Ind.Force
No.24 Squadron	4th	No.2(A.F.C.)Squadron	5th
No.25 Squadron	H.Q.	No.3(A.F.C.)Squadron	4th
No.27 Squadron	H.Q.	No.4(A.F.C.)Squadron	5th
No.29 Squadron	2nd	No.1 Balloon Co	1st
No.32 Squadron	H.Q.	No.2 Balloon Co	1st
No.35 Squadron	4th	No.3 Balloon Co	1st
No.40 Squadron	1st	No.4 Balloon Co	1st
No.41 Squadron	4th	No.5 Balloon Co	2nd
No.42 Squadron	5th	No.6 Balloon Co	2nd
No.43 Squadron	H.Q.	No.7 Balloon Co	2nd
No.46 Squadron	5th	No.8 Balloon Co	2nd
No.48 Squadron	4th	No.10 Balloon Co	1st
No.49 Squadron	H.Q.	No.11 Balloon Co	5th
No.52 Squadron	3rd	No.12 Balloon Co	3rd
No.53 Squadron	2nd	No.13 Balloon Co	4th
No.54 Squadron	H.Q.	No.14 Balloon Co	4th
No.55 Squadron	Ind.Force.	No.15 Balloon Co	H.Q.
No.56 Squadron	3rd	No.16 Balloon Co	4th
No.57 Squadron	3rd	No.17 Balloon Co	2nd
No.58 Squadron	H.Q.	No.18 Balloon Co	3rd
No.59 Squadron	3rd	No.19 Balloon Co	3rd
No.60 Squadron	3rd	No.20 Balloon Co	5th
No.62 Squadron	H.Q.		

8.5 Royal Air Force: Inter-war Years

The Royal Air Force carried out a wide variety of operations, both peaceable and offensive, between the end of the First World War and the beginning of the Second World War.

An example of the non-belligerent operations was the RAF involvement in pioneering work with regard to the planning and trial of air routes for civil airliners. The RAF undertook experiments with aircraft design and achieved various record successes with regard to altitude, long distance and other experimental flying. Many records concerning this aspect of the RAF's activities during this period can be found in AIR 2, AIR 5, AIR 8, and in the Operational Record Books in AIR 27 and AIR 29.

Offensive operations undertaken by the RAF, by both armoured cars and aircraft, occurred over much of the Empire as well as in countries that had been involved in the First World War. The Operational Record Books of Armoured Car Units can be found in AIR 29.

Operations in both North and South Russia continued until 1919 and numerous operations in Mesopotamia (later Iraq), Kurdistan, Persia (later Iran) and India went on sporadically until 1940.

In early 1920 the RAF was involved in operations in Somaliland, which finally led to the defeat of the 'Mad Mullah', who had been causing the British many problems since 1900.

Documents recording and describing the operations during this time are distributed amongst a number of different record series. AIR 1 contains numerous files relating to North and South Russia, Kurdistan and Mesopotamia. AIR 2 covers the same areas as AIR 1 and also holds files concerning Somaliland. AIR 5 contains files on Somaliland, Iraq and India.

Apart from operations in various parts of the world under the heading of 'Colonial Control', the RAF also undertook a variety of minor operations, explorations and survey flights. As already mentioned, many of the exploration and survey flights were very important as they pioneered routes for civilian passenger flights. Reports of these flights, surveys and operations can be found in AIR 5 and AIR 20. Each chapter is a separate activity. The reports are arranged in chronological order. The contents page of each volume tells you what the activity was, which officer was in command and when the activity occurred. All of the following are described as 'RAF Operations Flights and Surveys'.

Reference	Description	Date
AIR 5/820	Chapters 1–21	1919–27
AIR 5/821	Chapters 22–6	1927
AIR 5/822	Chapters 27–30	1927–8

AIR 5/823	Chapters 31–42	1928–9
AIR 5/824	Chapters 43–57	1929–30
AIR 5/825	Chapters 58–69	1930
AIR 5/826	Chapter 70	1930
AIR 5/1221	Chapters 71–4	1930–1
AIR 5/1222	Chapters 75–80a	1931
AIR 5/1223	Chapters 81–92	1931
AIR 5/1224	Chapter 93	1931–2
AIR 5/1225	Chapter 94–105	1932
AIR 5/1226	Chapters 106–16	1932–3
AIR 5/1228	Chapters 128–35	1933–4
AIR 5/1229	Chapters 136-43	1933-4
AIR 5/1230	Chapters 144–52	1934–5
AIR 20/453	Chapters 153–60	1935
AIR 20/454	Chapters 161–70	1935–6
AIR 20/455	Chapters 171–80	1935–7
AIR 20/456	Chapters 181–94	1936–7
AIR 20/457	Chapters 195–200	1937–8
AIR 20/459	Chapters 202–12	1938
AIR 20/460	Chapters 213–15	1938–9
AIR 20/461	Chapter 216	1938–9
AIR 20/462	Chapters 217–18	1938

8.5.1 *North and South Russia*

Reports on operations in South Russia can be found in AIR 1/408/15/232/6–8. The war diary for South Russia is in AIR 1/2375/226/11/1–5. Nominal rolls of other ranks and officers in the region are in AIR 1/1666/204/99/12 and 13 respectively.

Operational records from North Russia are in AIR 1/435/15/274/2–3 and AIR 1/438. Syren Force records can be found in AIR 1/472/15/312/167 and 168 and AIR 1/473/15/312/174.

Despatches covering operations in North and South Russia are in AIR 5/1340.

8.5.2 *Somaliland*

Operations by 12 DH 9as of the specially formed Z Unit RAF, against the 'Mad Mullah', were very important as they were the first independent operations undertaken by the RAF, in what was to be its prime role between 1918 and 1939, that of colonial policing.

References to this operation can be found in AIR 5/846, 1309–15 and 1422. (See Fig. 6 for the unit war diary in AIR 5/1309.) The files include operations orders, medical reports and photographs, observers' reports, a war diary (which interestingly lists all the jobs undertaken by the RAF airmen) and despatches.

Flight and Surveys

Chapters 31 - 42

1928 to 1929

31	Cairo to Cape Flight	F/Lt O.Gayford	1928
32	Search for lost shooting party in Libyan Desert	A.O.C., M.E.	30th Sept. - 5th Oct. 1928
33	Flight by 203 (F.B.) Sqdn Cattewater - Basrah	W/Cdr Howe	February - March 1929
34	Long Distance Flight Cranwell - Karachi	S/Ldr Jones Williams F/Lt Jenkins	24.4.1929 - 26.4.1929
35	Cairo - Cape Flight	S/Ldr C.R.Cox	1929
36	Flying Boat Cruise, Basra to Muscat	A/Cdr C.A.Burnett	May 1929
37	Flying Boat Cruise, Basra to Ras Al Khaimah	-	June 1929
38	Flight by Flying Boat of No.203 (F.B.) Squadron to India with Air Marshal Sir Geoffrey Salmond	-	August 1929
39	Singapore - Rangoon Flight	S/Ldr Livock	June 1929
40	Singapore - Calcutta Flight	S/Ldr Livock	August 1929
41	Singapore - Calcutta Flight	G/C Cave-Browne-Cave F/Lt Carnegie	September 1929
42	Singapore - Calcutta Flight	G/C Cave-Browne-Cave F/Lt Carnegie	October 1929

The medal roll for the Africa General Service Medal with Somaliland 1920 clasp is in AIR 2/2270. The recommendations for honours and awards granted for services during the operation can be found in AIR 2/204.

8.5.3 Mesopotamia

A summary of the campaign can be found in the National Archives in AIR 1/674/21/6/87. War diaries are in AIR 1/21/15/1/109, AIR 1/426/15/206/1 and AIR 1/432/15/260/23–25. A report by the Mesopotamia Commission on operations in the region is in AIR 1/2357/226/5/18.

Files of the RAF control of Mesopotamia are in AIR 5/224 and 476.

8.5.4 Kurdistan

Squadrons involved in operations in this region included 6, 30 and 63 Squadrons. Despatches concerning operations in this region in 1923 and 1924 can be found in AIR 1/2132/207/136/2 and AIR 5/292.

8.5.5 Iraq

Squadrons involved in various operations in Iraq included 6, 30, 55, 63, 70 and 84 Squadrons. Of all the operations in Iraq, the most significant occurred between 1928 and 1935. Most of the operational records concerning Iraq are in AIR 5. Of these the most significant are AIR 5/344, 460 and 544, AIR 5/1253–5 and AIR 5/1287–94. Squadron operational records can be found in AIR 27.

Photographs of southern Iraq between 1919 and 1929 can be found in AIR 5/842.

Unit records of a number of Armoured Car Companies which served in Iraq can be found in AIR 29/50–3.

8.5.6 India and Afghanistan

Numerous operations against various tribes in India and Afghanistan were undertaken between 1919 and 1940, with the majority occurring on the North West Frontier of India.

Organizational records of the RAF in India between 1918 and 1919 can be found in AIR 2/68, with a resumé of RFC operations in AIR 2/123.

A despatch from the Commander in Chief India, concerning the Third Afghan War in 1919, is in AIR 1/2132/207/136/1. Notes from war diaries of Waziristan Force 1919 and 1920 are in AIR 1/423/15/251/1.

Air operations which took place between 1922 and 1928 are covered in AIR 5/298.

A fuller history of all RAF operations in India can be found in AIR 5/1321–37.

Reports on India between 1921 and 1930, including a report from Air Vice Marshall Salmond, are in AIR 8/46. A memorandum on the use of air

Fig. 26 *A contents page of Chapters 31–42 of an RAF Flights and Surveys volume.* AIR 5/823

power in India is in AIR 8/83.

Records of operations on the North West Frontier of India between 1937 and 1939 are in AIR 8/529.

8.5.7 *Palestine*

Pre-war operations in Palestine covered the period 19 April 1936 to 3 September 1939. Numerous RAF units saw service in the region during this time. Of these, the following squadrons are known to have served there: 6, 14, 33, 80, 208, 211 and 216 Squadrons RAF.

A despatch concerning RAF operations in Palestine in 1936 is in AIR 2/1938. Monthly summaries of RAF activities between 1930 and 1939 are in AIR 5/1245–8, with further operational reports in AIR 5/1243–4.

Post-Second World War operations in Palestine are best sourced through the unit records in AIR 27.

8.6 Royal Air Force: Second World War and After

By the time of the Second World War, the organization of the RAF had evolved, and an understanding of the structure of the organization is necessary to make best use of the records.

Each of the Commands, for example Fighter and Bomber, was broken down into 'Groups', which in most cases were based around a given geographical area. Certain units of a similar type, sorted either by task (Strike Wing, Banff) or specialization (Balloon, Signals, etc.), could be gathered together under a 'Wing'. At the lower end of this chain of command was the Squadron.

An example of the chain is given below.

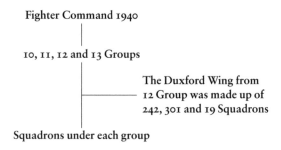

Operational records of the RAF between 1939 and 1945 can be found in a number of different sources. The records listed below are primarily those operational records where information concerning individuals may be found. Those in this section are more useful in gaining a general knowledge of operations.

As part of King's Regulations of the RAF it was a requirement that all commands, groups, stations, wings, squadrons and all miscellaneous units had to complete RAF Forms 540 and 541. Forms 540 were for monthly summaries and were completed by all units. Forms 541 were for daily summaries and were completed by units such as RAF squadrons.

Records which cover more than just specific units or organizations include Combat Reports in AIR 50, which are arranged by unit and include a number of Fleet Air Arm squadrons and other non-RAF units. The records in AIR 50 have been digitized and placed on DocumentsOnline. It is possible to search AIR 50 on DocumentsOnline by name or squadron. Anything found in AIR 50 this way can be downloaded (for a fee external to the TNA building).

Intelligence records concerning RAF operations, especially those with Special Forces, can be found in AIR 40 and AIR 20.

The records of the Central Interpretation Unit can be found in the series AIR 34, which is full of photographs of targets either before or after attack, as well as many other images used for intelligence work. The series not only consists of Interpretation and Monthly Summaries throughout the war: the unit's own 'Evidence in Camera' series of publications, all of which contain photographs, can also be found here.

There are numerous records relating to a variety of specific as well as general operations distributed amongst the AIR record series. At the end of the war a number of narratives relating to air operations were compiled and these can be found in AIR 41.

The records of the 2nd Tactical Air Force, which was responsible for operations from airfields in northwestern Europe after D-Day, are in AIR 37.

8.6.1 *Commands*

As commands were the highest link in the administrative chain of command in the sole hands of the RAF, they kept separate records rather than just Operational Record Books (ORBs). The table below shows where these command papers are now located.

Command	Reference
Balloon Command	AIR 13
Bomber Command	AIR 14
Coastal Command	AIR 15
Fighter Command	AIR 16
Maintenance Command	AIR 17
Overseas Commands	AIR 23
Air Training Command	AIR 32
Ferry and Transport Command	AIR 38
Army Co-operation Command	AIR 39

Of all of these commands, the records of those actually involved in operations are the most expansive and extensive. When completing research into a particular incident it may be necessary to consult the Command papers for certain details.

The ORBs of commands can be found in AIR 24 and are arranged alphabetically by name of command and then chronologically under each command. Included in AIR 24 are the record books of the Director of the Women's Auxiliary Air Force. The Operational Record Books in AIR 24 cover not only the obvious commands such as Bomber, Fighter and Coastal Command, but also cover many others. A list of the commands and organizations found in AIR 24 can be found in Appendix 5.

8.6.2 Groups

The ORBs of RAF groups are in AIR 25. These records are arranged numerically by number of the group, and the type of group, be it a fighter or bomber group, for example, is mentioned in the series list.

8.6.3 Wings

The ORBs for wings can be found in AIR 26. These records are arranged in numerical order by the number of the wing. However, the series list does note the type of wing, whether it be a fighter, signal or overseas wing, for example. Apart from a few instances individuals are rarely mentioned.

In many instances wings fed information relating to operations up the chain of command through group and up to command. It is therefore possible to find the activities of wings in group and command records.

8.6.4 Squadrons

Squadron ORBs are by far the most informative of all RAF unit records. These books record the sorties of each unit, giving the aircraft type, unit call-sign or aircraft serial number, crew (by name), task or target, weapon load, time of take-off and time of return. If the aircraft did not return, this is also recorded. The arrival and departure of personnel joining and leaving the unit is usually recorded, as are details concerning awards.

The records in AIR 27 can be used to create a list of all the flying operations that RAF aircrew completed.

Fig. 27 *Location of RAF squadrons in June 1941, showing where a given squadron was and what it was flying.* AIR 10/3955

Squadron Operational Record Books for the South African Air Force can also be found in the series AIR 54.

Operational records concerning units (138 and 161 squadrons) who flew on behalf of SOE (Special Operations Executive) can be found in AIR 20.

A typical example of an RAF squadron ORB can be seen in Fig. 28.

No. 11 Group. Uxbridge

Station.	Unit.	Equipment.
Biggin Hill	No. 92 (East India)	}Spitfire.
	No. 609	
Castle Camps	—	—
Croydon	—	
Debden	No. 601	}Hurricane.
	No. 3	
Ford	No. 23	Havoc I.
	F.I.U.	Blenheim.
Gravesend	No. 74	Spitfire.
Hawkinge	No. 91	Spitfire.
Hendon	No. 24	Various.
	No. 116 Calibration	Lysander.
	No. 1 Camouflage Unit	Various.
Hornchurch	No. 54	}Spitfire.
	No. 603	
Hunsdon	No. 85	Havoc I.
Kenley	No. 258	}Hurricane.
	No. 302 (Polish)	
Manston	—	—
Martlesham	No. 71 (Eagle)	Hurricane.
Northolt	No. 303 (Polish)	Spitfire.
	No. 306 (Polish)	Hurricane.
North Weald	No. 56	Hurricane.
Redhill	No. 1	Hurricaue.
Southend	No. 611	Spitfire.
Stapleford Tawney	No. 242 (Canadian Pilots)	Hurricane.
Tangmere	No. 145	Spitfire.
	No. 219	Blenheim/Beaufighter.
	No. 610	}Spitfire.
	No. 616	
West Malling	No. 29	Beaufighter.
	No. 264	Defiant.

OPERATIONS RECORD BOOK.

Appendix.................Air Force (India) Form. 541.

DETAIL OF WORK CARRIED OUT.

From.....hrs...../...../.....to.....hrs...../...../.....   By. NO. 159 SQUADRON. R.A.F.   No. of pages used for day.................

Aircraft Type and No	Crew.	Duty.	Time Up.	Time Down.	Remarks.	References.
Liberator BZ.922."S". Night 4/5th Feb:1944.	"A" Flight. S/Ldr. C.G. Clegg P/O. F.P.A. Heynert W/O. J.N.Culleten F/O.J.R.Fullerten DFM F/O.G.A.Gewing F/O.R.W.Ustick (F/C) W/O.A.N.Webb F/Sgt.J.Harris W/Cdr.Winfield AFC.	Capt: Co-p: Nav: 1stWop: 2ndWop: M.U. B.G. R.G. Pass.	21.44	06.26	ATTACKING HE-HO Aerodrome. Lead: 1st stick. 1x1000 GPTD..C25- 3x500 GPTD..C25 01.18 hrs.; 160 I.A.S., 300 Mag. 2nd stick 5x500 GPTD..C25- 01.27 hrs.; 12,700 ft., 160 I.A.S., 260 Mag. First stick aimed at N-S. runway, level. Second stick aimed at N-S. runway, level. First and second runs: bursts seen but not pin-pointed.	See APPENDIX A Page 1.
Liberator BZ.982."T" Night 4/5th Feb:1944.	F/Lt.E.I.D.Stanley. W/O.J.W. Falconer. F/Lt.T.J.O'Donehue DFM.Nav: F/Sgt.R. King F/Sgt.J.D.Lemas. W/O. D.J.Ryan. (F/C) Sgt.S.W.Chalcraft W/O.J.W.F.King. F/O.C.J.Temlin	Capt: Co-p: Nav: 1stWop: 2ndWop: M.U. B.G. R.G. 2ndNav:	21.32	05.48	Attacking HE-HO Aerodrome. Lead: 10x500 GPTD..C25- 01.26 hrs., 11,200 ft. 160 IAS. All bombs dropped in one stick. 135 Mag. Aimed at S. end of N-S runway. Four bombs seen to burst across runway and rest in dispersal area.	"
Liberator BZ.897 "Z" Night 4/5th Feb: 1944.	F/O.R.L.H.McDougall W/O.T.H. Morris. Sgt.A.J.Withers. F/Lt.D.I.C.Beissier. F/Sgt.J. Brown F/Sgt.L.J.H.Talbot F/Sgt.W. Hendry(F/C) F/Sgt.D. Stokoe F/Sgt.J.P. Goodisen	Capt: Co-p: F/Eng: Nav: 1stWop: 2ndWop: M.U. B.G. R.G.	21.40	06.50	Attacking HE-HO Aerodrome. Lead: 1st stick. As for a/c "A". 01.25 hrs. 12,500 ft. 165 IAS, 255 Mag. 2nd stick. As for a/c "A". 01.32 hrs. 12,500 ft. 165 IAS, 265 Mag. First stick: aimed at intersection of runways. Second stick: aimed at intersection of runways. Both runs, bursts seen, but positions not pin-pointed.	"
Liberator BZ. 960 "V" Night 4/5th Feb: 1944.	F/Sgt.C.A. King F/Sgt.J. Barritt Sgt.N.J. Davis W/O.J.E. Bell F/Sgt.J.McGregor F/Sgt.McLaughlin P/O.D.M. Black (F/C) F/Sgt.W.McCaffery W/O.F.J.S.J.Edwards	Capt: Co-p: F/Eng: Nav: 1stWop: 2ndWop: M.U. B.G. R.G.	21.51½	05.53	Attacking HE-HO Aerodrome. Lead: 1st stick. 10x500 GPTD..C25. 0110 hrs. 12,000 ft. 160 IAS, 255 Mag. dropped in two sticks, 5 each, level. 0115 hrs. 12,000 ft. 160 IAS, 305 Mag. First stick aimed at N-S runway. Second stick aimed at N-S runway. First run bursts not seen. Second run, bursts seen across N. end of N-S runway.	"

8.6.5 Stations

The station ORBs are in AIR 28 and are arranged in alphabetical order. The AIR 28 series list contains an alphabetical index. Station 540s record numerous incidents which affected them, and in many cases it is in the station ORB that details concerning Courts of Inquiry may be found. Individuals are frequently mentioned in station ORBs.

Photographs of RAF air stations can be found in AIR 20/7585 (A–I) and AIR 20/7586 (K–Z).

8.6.6 Other units

The ORBs of all those RAF units that may be called miscellaneous but are no less important can be found in AIR 29. Amongst the units to be found in AIR 29 are RAF regiments, air sea rescue flights, operational training and conversion units and other flying training units.

8.6.7 Since 1945

Researching records for post-1945 operations can be done by consulting the series lists for all of those records which covered the Second World War or by using the Catalogue. Numerous records exist for operations in Malaya, Korea, Borneo, the Middle East and Kenya. The squadron records in AIR 27 and other units in AIR 29 all contain records of this period.

Perhaps some of the most interesting records concerning post-1945 RAF operations are those connected with the testing of atomic weapons. Some of the files concerning tests in Australia and on Christmas Island are still retained by the MOD, but most can be located by using the search term 'Grapple'.

Fig. 28 (facing) *WW2 RAF Squadron crew list typical of one always recorded in an Operational Record Book.* AIR 27/1061

Fig. 29 (right) *RAF operations report for the Malayan Emergency 1949.* AIR 23/8443

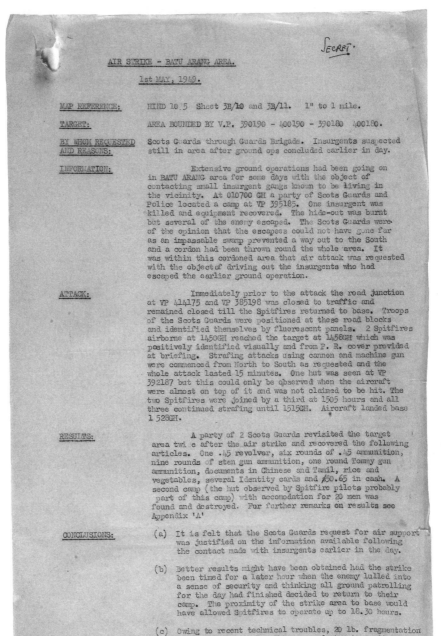

SECRET.

AIR STRIKE - BATU ARANG AREA.

1st MAY, 1949.

MAP REFERENCE: HIND 10.5 Sheet 3B/10 and 3B/11. 1" to 1 mile.

TARGET: AREA BOUNDED BY V.P. 390190 - 400190 - 390180 400180.

BY WHOM REQUESTED AND REASONS: Scots Guards through Guards Brigade. Insurgents suspected still in area after ground ops concluded earlier in day.

INFORMATION: Extensive ground operations had been going on in BATU ARANG area for some days with the object of contacting small insurgent gangs known to be living in the vicinity. At 010700 GH a party of Scots Guards and Police located a camp at VP 395185. One insurgent was killed and equipment recovered. The hide-out was burnt but several of the enemy escaped. The Scots Guards were of the opinion that the escapees could not have gone far as an impassable swamp prevented a way out to the South and a cordon had been thrown round the whole area. It was within this cordoned area that air attack was requested with the object of driving out the insurgents who had escaped the earlier ground operation.

ATTACK: Immediately prior to the attack the road junction at VP 414175 and VP 385198 was closed to traffic and remained closed till the Spitfires returned to base. Troops of the Scots Guards were positioned at these road blocks and identified themselves by fluorescent panels. 2 Spitfires airborne at 1450GH reached the target at 1458GH which was positively identified visually and from P. R. cover provided at briefing. Strafing attacks using cannon and machine gun were commenced from North to South as requested and the whole attack lasted 15 minutes. One hut was seen at VP 392187 but this could only be observed when the aircraft were almost on top of it and was not claimed to be hit. The two Spitfires were joined by a third at 1505 hours and all three continued strafing until 1515GH. Aircraft landed base 1 528GH.

RESULTS: A party of 2 Scots Guards revisited the target area twice after the air strike and recovered the following articles. One .45 revolver, six rounds of .45 ammunition, nine rounds of sten gun ammunition, one round Tommy gun ammunition, documents in Chinese and Tamil, rice and vegetables, several Identity cards and £50.65 in cash. A second camp (the hut observed by Spitfire pilots probably part of this camp) with accomodation for 20 men was found and destroyed. For further remarks on results see Appendix 'A'

CONCLUSIONS: (a) It is felt that the Scots Guards request for air support was justified on the information available following the contact made with insurgents earlier in the day.

(b) Better results might have been obtained had the strike been timed for a later hour when the enemy lulled into a sense of security and thinking all ground patrolling for the day had finished decided to return to their camp. The proximity of the strike area to base would have allowed Spitfires to operate up to 18.30 hours.

(c) Owing to recent technical troubles, 20 lb. fragmentation bombs were not used. This was unfortunate as it is considered that the small anti-personnel bomb now being carried by Spitfires produces the maximum effectiveness in clearing jungle covered country and is much disliked by insurgents when caught in such an attack.

8.7 Fleet Air Arm

The formal return to Admiralty control of the Fleet Air Arm (FAA) just prior to the Second World War means that operational records of the service may be found in the ADM and AIR record series, as described in the following sections.

8.7.1 Second World War

Operational records of the FAA are primarily to be found in four Admiralty record series (ADM 1, ADM 116, ADM 199 and ADM 207) and two Air Ministry record series (AIR 27, AIR 50).

ORBs of some FAA squadrons can be found in ADM 207. However, the series does not have all of the FAA ORBs. These records usually note the sorties, crew, and hours flown on sorties, and many contain additional notes relating to operations. A number of FAA ORBs can be found in AIR 27/2386 and 2387.

Reports of proceedings of FAA squadrons can be found in ADM 199. Rather than being completed on a day-to-day basis as ORBs were, the reports of proceedings were compiled from a number of different sources and accompanied by an overview from the commanding officer. The reports of proceedings only covered a short duration; consequently it may be necessary to obtain a number of these reports to create a complete operational history of a unit. A report of proceedings concerning the attack on Taranto can be found in ADM 199/167.

In many cases the activities of FAA squadrons can also be found by locating the records of the ships from which they operated. Many of these reports can be found in ADM 199. A report concerning the sinking of the *Bismarck* and the involvement of 818 and 820 squadrons can found by looking at the report written by the CO of HMS *Ark Royal* in ADM 199 /657.

Ships' logs, which contain very brief details about operational activities, can be found in ADM 53.

Reports concerning specific operations or events such as the attack on Taranto or the sinking of the *Bismarck* may be found in ADM 1, Series 1, Codes 3 and 90, and ADM 116, Codes 3 and 90. Reports concerning the attack on Taranto can be found in ADM 1/11182, ADM 223/336 and ADM 234/325.

Many operations during the Second World War were given codenames which can be used to identify relevant records, if they are known to the researcher. The FAA attack on Taranto was codenamed 'Judgement' and the FAA attack on the *Tirpitz* in April 1944 was codenamed 'Tungsten'. Records concerning Operation Tungsten can be found in ADM 1/15695, ADM 1/15806, ADM 199/941 and ADM 237/345.

OPERATION JUDGEMENT.

CREW LIST.

FIRST STRIKING FORCE.

Aircraft.	Pilot.	Observer.
L4A	Lt. Comdr. K. WILLIAMSON, R.N.	Lieut. N.J. SCARLETT, R.N.
L4C	S/Lt.(A) P.D.J. SPARKE, DSC.RN.	S/Lt. (A) J.W. NEALE, R.N.
L4R	S/Lt. (A) A.S.D. MACAULAY, R.N.	S/Lt.(A) A.L.O. WRAY, RNVR.
L4K	Lt. N.McI. KEMP, R.N.	S/Lt.(A) R.A. BAILEY, R.N.
L4M	Lt. (A) H.I.A. SWAYNE, R.N.	S/Lt.(A) J. BUSCALL, RNVR.
E4F	*Lt. M.R. MAUND, R.N.	*S/Lt.(A) W.A. BULL, R.N.
L4P	Lt. (A) L. J. KIGGELL, R.N.	Lt. H.R.B. JANVRIN, R.N.
L5B	Lt. (A) C.B. LAMB, R.N.	*Lieut. K.C. GRIEVE, R.N.
E5A	*Capt. O. PATCH, R.M.	*Lieut. D.G. GOODWIN, R.N.
L4L	S/Lt. (A) W.C. SARRA, R.N.	Mid. (A) J. BOWKER, R.N.
L4H	S/Lt. (A) A.J. FORDE, R.N.	S/Lt. (A) A.MARDEL-FERREIRA, RNVR.
E5Q	*Lt. (A) J.B. MURRAY, R.N.	*S/Lt. (A) S.M. PAINE, R.N.

SECOND STRIKING FORCE.

Aircraft.	Pilot.	Observer.
L5A	Lieut. Comdr. J.W. HALE, R.N.	Lieut. G.A. CARLINE, R.N.
E4H	*Lieut. G.W. BAYLY, R.N.	*Lieut. H.J. SLAUGHTER, R.N.
L5H	Lieut. (A) C.S.C. LEA, R.N.	S/Lt. (A) P.D. JONES, R.N.
L5K	Lt. F.M.A. TORRENS-SPENCE, R.N.	Lieut. A.W.F. SUTTON, R.N.
E5H	*Lt.(A) J.W.G. WELHAM, R.N.	*Lt. P. HUMPHREYS, E.G.M. R.N.
L5B	Lieut. R.W.V. HAMILTON, R.N.	S/Lt. (A) J.R. WEEKES, R.N.
L4F	Lieut. (A) R.G. SKELTON, R.N.	S/Lt. (A) E.A. PERKINS, RNVR.
L5F	Lieut. E.W. CLIFFORD, R.N.	Lieut. G.R.M. GOING, R.N.
L5Q	Lieut. (A) W.D. MORFORD, R.N.	S/Lt. (A) R.A. FGREEN, R.N.

* - Officers of H.M.S. "EAGLE". Remainder from H.M.S. "ILLUSTRIOUS".

92

(Page 5 of Commanding Officer, H.M.S. "ILLUSTRIOUS"'s No.2715/1097 dated 13th November 1940.)

- -

(vii) <u>Kiggell/Janvrin.</u>

Task: To drop flares along the eastern shore and S.A.P. bombs on any convenient target.

The aircraft was detached by the Squadron Commander off Cape San Vito and came in at 7500 feet. Over Cape San Vito and the promintory H.E. A.A. fire was encountered. Commencing at 2302 a line of eight flares was dropped at half mile intervals set to burn at 4500 feet. After the flares had been dropped and appeared to be providing satisfactory illumination, the pilot turned to starboard and cruised around for 15-20 minutes looking for a target, and then made a dive bombing attack on the most southerly oil storage depot from which a pipe line leads to the new jetty. No results were observed. 'get away' was made at 2325 in a southerly direction. "ILLUSTRIOUS" was sighted at 0112 and the aircraft landed on at 0120.

(viii) <u>Lamb/Grieve.</u>

Task: Stand by flare dropper.

Came in astern of Kiggell/Janvrin but as the first flares appeared satisfactory no flares were dropped. The course flown and the A.A. fire experienced was the same as that by Kiggell/Janvrin and the same oil storage depot was the target for a dive bombing attack but no results were observed.

(ix) <u>Patch/Goodwin.</u>

Task: Dive bombing attack on the line of cruisers and destroyers moored stem on against the quay side on the south of the Mar Piccolo.

The aircraft came in at 8500 feet over San Pietro Island at 2306, encountering fire from both Islands and from Rondinella Point, crossed the Mar Grande and the canal and to the middle of the western portion of the Mar Piccolo. Difficulty was experienced at first in identifying the target which appeared to be in a shadow but two minutes after crossing the canal the target was identified and a dive bombing attack was made from 1500 feet obliquely across two cruisers from N.W. to S.E. at 2315. Pom pom fire from a number of points along the quay side, and from the cruisers in the Mar Piccolo was encountered. The pilot then turned east and about five minutes later a large fire was observed from the direction of the seaplane base. Further anti-aircraft fire was met from a point near the village of San Gorgio but this was avoided by diving behind the neighbouring range of hills. The aircraft crossed the coast in a southerly direction some 8 miles east of Taranto harbour. "ILLUSTRIOUS" was sighted at 0135 and landed on at 0155.

(x) . . . .

An example of an FAA squadron's report of proceedings (ADM 199 /167) can be seen in Fig. 31 above.

Since 1945

FAA operational records after 1945 can be found in the record series used for Second World War records, but they are primarily to be found in ADM 1 and ADM 116. A new post-war record series, ADM 335 Fleet Air Arm Operational Records, also contains material of the post-war era up to the 1960s.

8.8 Glider Pilot Regiment and Army Air Corps: Second World War and After

As the dual role of the Glider Pilot Regiment (GPR) and Army Air Corps (AAC) covered both the air and ground, records relating to their operational activities may be found in both AIR and WO record series. In some cases the activities of these units were controlled by Headquarters Combined Operations, whose records can be found in DEFE 2.

As units of the GPR and AAC had specific titles and they took part in military operations which were given codenames, it is these which can be used to identify and obtain records concerning their activities in the Second World War.

Operational Record Books of AAC Air Observation Post (AOP) squadrons can be found in AIR 27. AOP squadrons were numbered between 651 and 660. Further details about the numbering of AOP squadrons can be found in *RAF Squadrons* by C.G. Jefford.

Operational Record Books of glider units, including squadrons and training units, can be found in AIR 29.

Unit War Diaries of Army units in the Second World War are arranged by operational theatre and then by unit. A number of diaries concerning glider units can be found in WO 166 (Home Forces), WO 169 (North Africa), WO 170 (Italy) and WO 171 (North Western Europe).

Operations which involved the GPR include Operation Freshman (the attempted attack on a heavy water plant at Vermortt in Norway), Operation Husky (the invasion of Sicily), Operation Overlord (the Normandy invasion), Operation Market Garden (the airborne landing at Arnhem) and Operation Varsity (the crossing of the Rhine). There are numerous files concerning the GPR/AAC part in these operations, but some of the most significant are listed below.

8.8.1 *Freshman*
The main records can be found in AIR 20/3648, 4527 and 11930, AIR 39/45 and 147, DEFE 2/219–24 and 1408 and HS 2/184. For the records concerning the war crimes committed in connection with this operation see 12.3.

8.8.2 *Husky*

The main records can be found in AIR 8/1315 and 1316, AIR 20/2585 and 4475–7, AIR 23/5527, WO 106/3877, WO 201/659 and WO 204/1072.

8.8.3 *Overlord*

There are thousands of files concerning the Normandy invasion. Those applicable to the GPR include WO 205/78–80, WO 219/222–6 and WO 219/2180.

8.8.4 *Market Garden*

The main records can be found in AIR 37/1214 and 1249, AIR 67/32 and WO 205/870.

8.8.5 *Varsity*

The main records can be found in AIR 14/1438, AIR 20/4314, AIR 37/56, 57, 267, 268, 304, 305, 326, 327, 543, 907, 909 and 1128, WO 106/5847, WO 205/200–4, 951 and 952.

The Aircrew Log Book of Staff Sergeant D.W. Lee, 1 Battalion Glider Pilot Regiment, can be found in AIR 4/59.

8.8.6 *Since 1945*

Post-war activities of the AAC can once again be found in AIR 27 and WO 233. The papers of the Sixth Airborne Division in Palestine between 1945 and 1948, which included men of the AAC, may be found in WO 275. Other operational records can be found in the Quarterly Historical Reports in WO 261–71 and the Unit Records in WO 305, most of which can be searched by unit on the Catalogue.

9 CASUALTIES AND AIR CRASHES

9.1 Casualties

Loss of life, through flying accidents or through enemy action, is unfortunately a common occurrence in the history of aviation. The following records, whilst recording the demise of thousands of individuals, do at least enable researchers to create a more complete picture of the career of a member of the flying services.

In some cases it is possible to find files concerning the loss of a particular aircraft by searching the Catalogue by the aircraft type and/or serial number and this is especially so of Fleet Air Arm aircraft in the 1950s and 1960s.

9.1.1 *First World War*

Information concerning commissioned and warrant officers and ratings who died from whatever cause, be it illness or through enemy action, can be found in ADM 242. There is an officers' card index in the Document Reading Room, ADM 242/1–6. This is arranged alphabetically and shows name, date, place and cause of death. The War Graves roll in ADM 242/7–10, covering all ranks, gives rank or rating, date of birth, date and place of death and the name and address of next of kin.

Numerous files concerning casualties can be found in AIR 1 by using the keyword 'casualties' on the Catalogue. Amongst the files to be found are many concerning officers who are missing, presumed dead.

Dead of the RFC and RAF can be found by using *Soldiers Died in the Great War*, which is available on CD-ROM in the Library. The second source to consult is *Airmen Died in the Great War* by Chris Hobson, a copy of which is available in the Library. To find out where an individual is buried or commemorated, try using the Commonwealth War Graves Commission website (*www.cwgc.org*) and search their online registers.

The RAF Museum holds a number of casualty cards concerning RFC and RAF casualties of the First World War. In many cases a card will provide the unit, date and place of death and other basic biographical data.

See 15.6 for details on the RAF Museum.

Statistics of casualties incurred by the RFC/RAF during the First World War can be found in AIR 1/39/15/7. A list of Americans who died whilst serving with the RFC/RAF can be found in AIR 2/219. A list of casualties, both military and civil, incurred during air raids and shore bombardments between December 1914 and June 1918 can be found in AIR 1/604/16/15/235.

French or Belgian death certificates of men who died in France or Belgium but outside of the area of operations can be found in RG 35/45–9.

9.1.2   *Inter-war years*

Specific casualty records for the inter-war years (1919–38) are not easily located. If a death occurred in a given unit, you can consult the unit records to see if anything is mentioned. The casualty records of the Royal Navy, and therefore the Fleet Air Arm, continue after the First World War in ADM 104. In ADM 104/144–8 the registers of reports of deaths of naval ratings up to 1929 can be found. The Commonwealth War Graves Commission does hold some data relating to deaths between 1919 and 1938.

9.1.3   *Second World War*

During the Second World War over 55,000 aircrew lost their lives as a result of enemy action, in accidents or through other circumstances. An initial consultation of the Commonwealth War Graves Commission records, either by letter or by using their website (see 15.7), will provide the researcher with much useful data. Beyond name, rank, date of death and place of commemoration or burial, the CWGC records may also provide the researcher with the all-important unit details. Once a unit is identified, then the relevant unit and operational records can be consulted (see chapter 8).

Unit operational records may provide not only personal details but also the cause of death, be it in action or otherwise. As there were so many flying accidents during the Second World War, very few of the accident inquiry records have survived. Depending upon the location of the accident, it may be possible to find brief details in the RAF Station Operational Record Books in AIR 28.

Doing a keyword search on the 'Online Lists' using the term 'Casualty' or 'Casualties' will produce plenty of results. An example of a record that could be found as a result of such a search is AIR 16/609, which contains the 'Aircrew casualty statistics for Battle of Britain'.

The Roll of Honour for Army deaths in the Second World War is in WO 304. This roll is arranged in alphabetical order and the information contained in it is numerically coded. An explanatory guide to these codes is available in the WO 304 paper Catalogue. WO 304 has been digitized and

Fig. 32 (facing) *Combat report of Captain Baron von Richthofen Sept 17, 1916.* AIR 1/686/21/13/2250

1st Victory.

Sept. 17.1916.
Vickers Nr.7018.   Motor No.701.   Machine guns
                                                 Nos.17314, 10372.
near Villers Plouich.   11 a.m.

When patrol flying I detected shrapnel clouds in
direction Cambrai. I hurried forth and met a squad which I
attacked shortly after 11 a.m. I singled out the last
machine and fired several times at closest range (10 meters).
Suddenly the enemy propeller stood stock still. The machine
went down gliding and I followed until I had killed the
observer who had not stopped shooting until the last moment.

Now my opponent went downwards in sharp curves. In
approx. 1200 meters a second German machine came along and
attacked my victim right down to the ground and then landed
next to the English plane.

                                        Frhr. v. Richthofen.

                                                Lieut.

Witnesses: Capt. Boelke from above and Capt.Gaede,
             Lieut.Pelser and other officers from below.

Pilot: N.C.O. Rees, wounded, hospital at Cambrai.

Observer: Killed, buried by Jagdstaffel 4.

2nd Victory.

Sept. 23, 1916.
11 a.m.
One seater Martinsyde, G.W. Nr. 174.

----

11 a.m. air fight above Bapaume. Adversary dashed,
after 300 shots, mortally wounded, near Bengny (Street
Bapaume - Cambrai) to ground.

Two machine guns recovered, will be delivered.

Dead Inmate buried by 7th Infantry Division.

                                        Frhr. v. Richthofen.

all of the coded data turned into plain English. It is possible to access the Army Roll of Honour via the published sources section on the public computers on the first floor of the National Archives.

Casualty records of the Royal Navy and consequently the Fleet Air Arm are in ADM 104/127–39 and cover deaths from September 1939–June 1948. Once again these records are arranged alphabetically.

The RAF Museum at Hendon holds a number of casualty cards relating to 1939–1945. For more information about accessing the RAF Museum archive see 15.6.

9.1.4 *Since 1945*

Very few specific casualty records for the post-1945 period are yet available. By far the most useful sources are the operational records. See chapter 8 for further details.

9.2 Air Crashes

Although there are policy files concerning air crashes in a number of different AIR and AVIA record series, the records in AVIA 5, Ministry of Aviation Accident Investigation Branch, contain detailed reports about crashes involving military aircraft from 1919 to the post-Second World War period. The records in AVIA 5 provide aircraft serial number and type, names of crew and a detailed analysis of the cause of the crash with appropriate recommendations. If you know the serial number of the aircraft involved in a particular crash you can use it as a keyword to search the Catalogue.

The Admiralty also carried out investigations into their crashed aircraft. However, unlike the records in AVIA 5, the records in ADM 1 only really cover the post-1945 period. This is because prior to the Second World War the aircraft of the Royal Navy were administered by the RAF. As with AVIA 5 you can use an aircraft serial number as a keyword when searching the Catalogue.

10 MEDALS AND AWARDS

Medals can be split into a number of different groups depending upon the purpose for which they were awarded. In this chapter it is intended to describe the three most important groups and the records associated with them.

For a full description of medal-related records held by the National Archives and in the India Office collection at the British Library see *Medals: The Researcher's Guide* by William Spencer.

10.1 Royal Engineers Balloon Section: Campaign Medals

Campaign medals are those medals that are awarded to an individual for being present in a theatre of operations and in some cases, taking part in particular battles. Sometimes a medal only was issued denoting which campaign an individual was involved in. In lengthier campaigns it was also possible to receive clasps to a medal, denoting particular places or dates where and when an individual was involved. There are a variety of different

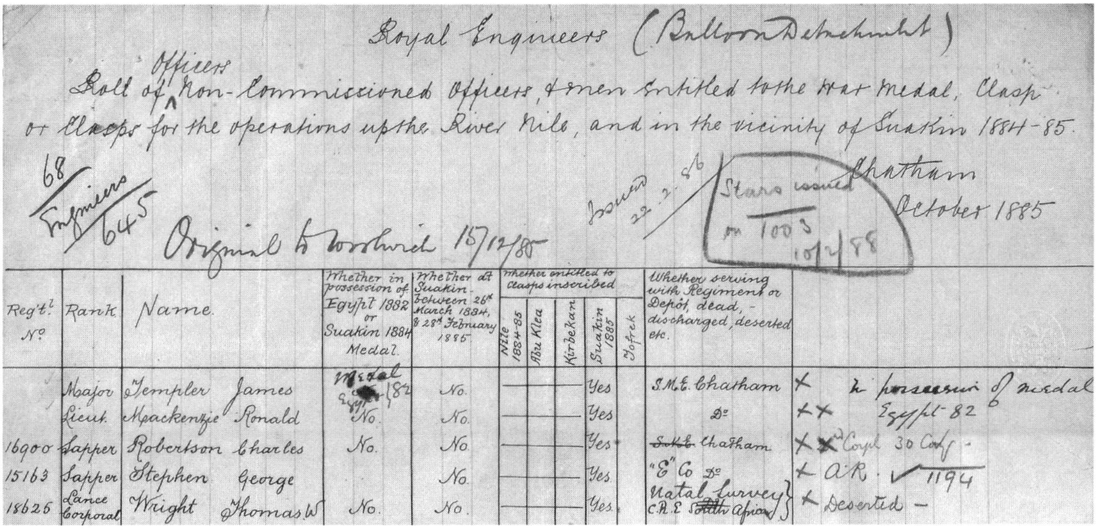

Royal Engineers (Balloon Detachment)

Roll of Officers Non-Commissioned Officers, & men entitled to the War Medal, Clasp or Clasps for the operations up the River Nile, and in the vicinity of Suakin 1884-85.

68 Engineers 645

Original to Woolwich 15/12/85

Issued 22.2.86

Stars issued on 1003 10/2/88

Chatham October 1885

Regt.l No.	Rank	Name		Whether in possession of Egypt 1882 or Suakin 1884 Medal	Whether at Suakin between 26th March 1884, & 28th February 1885	Whether entitled to clasps inscribed: Nile 1884-85	Abu Klea	Kirbekan	Suakin 1885	Tofrek	Whether serving with Regiment or Depot, dead, discharged, deserted etc.	
	Major	Templer	James	Medal Egypt 1882	No.				Yes		S.M.E. Chatham	× In possession of medal
	Lieut.	Mackenzie	Ronald	No.	No.				Yes		Do	×× Egypt 82
16900	Sapper	Robertson	Charles	No.	No.				Yes		S.M.E. Chatham	×× Corpl 30 Coy
15163	Sapper	Stephen	George		No.				Yes		"E" Co Do	× A.R. ✓ 1194
18626	Lance Corporal	Wright	Thomas W	No.	No.				Yes		Natal Survey C.R.E. South Africa	× Deserted –

Fig. 33 *The Egypt Medal Roll with the clasp Suakin 1885 granted to members of the RE Balloon Section.* WO 100/64 F80–1

campaign medals that have been issued for numerous campaigns since 1793. As British military aviation is a comparatively new part of warfare, so the campaigns in which aviation first took part are quite recent.

The varied sources of manpower recruited for the RE Balloon Section, and more importantly the Royal Flying Corps, Royal Naval Air Service and Royal Air Force, meant that many members of these organizations saw active service with other units prior to becoming involved in aviation. Many men received campaign and other medals with their previous units. These awards are not discussed here. For more information about medals awarded to members of the British Army see *Army Records: A Guide for Family Historians* by William Spencer, and for those with a Royal Navy or Royal Marine background see *Tracing your Naval Ancestors* by B. Pappalardo.

Prior to the formation of the RFC in 1912, all campaign service was undertaken by the Royal Engineers Balloon Section. Although this section was involved in a number of different military operations around the world prior to 1912, its men were only awarded campaign medals for three different campaigns.

The first campaign medal men of the RE Balloon Section were awarded was the Egypt Medal 1882–9, for services in eastern Sudan in 1885. The roll for this medal can be found in WO 100/64 ff80. The medal roll lists the name, rank and number of all those men of the section who were entitled to the medal.

After service in the eastern Sudan, the next campaign in which balloons were involved was the South African or Boer War 1899–1902. Three sections of balloons took part in the war, all of those men who served in South Africa being awarded the Queen's South Africa Medal. The medal rolls for this medal can be found in WO 100/160. Not only does the medal roll list the names of those who were eligible for the medal, it also notes the particular clasps an individual was entitled to, thereby signifying where in South Africa he served.

The third and final campaign which resulted in men of the RE Balloon Section being awarded a campaign medal was the Boxer Rebellion or Third China War in 1900. As the majority of their resources were in use in South Africa, the number of RE Balloon Section men who saw service in China was very small. The medal roll for the Third China Medal can be found in WO 100/95.

10.2 Royal Flying Corps: Campaign Medals

Medal rolls relating to campaign medals won by members of the Royal Flying Corps are restricted to two record series: WO 100 for non-First

World War medal records, and WO 329 for First World War campaign medal rolls.

10.2.1 *First World War medals and Silver War Badge*

Six different campaign medals were awarded for service during the First World War and, apart from in exceptional cases, the maximum number of medals which could be awarded to an individual was three. The medals were: the 1914 Star, the 1914/15 Star, the British War Medal 1914–20, the Victory Medal 1914–19, the Territorial Force War Medal 1914–19 and the Mercantile Marine War Medal. The last named medal was awarded exclusively to members of the Merchant Navy, and although really outside of the scope of this book, it may be possible to find men of the RFC, RNAS and RAF who qualified for the medal prior to joining the armed forces.

The 1914 Star, authorized in 1917, was awarded for service in France and Belgium between 5 August and 22 November 1914. In 1919 a bar with the inscription '5th Aug.–22nd Nov. 1914' was sanctioned. Only those personnel who had actually been under fire during the above specified dates were eligible. The 1914 Star was not awarded on its own; it should always be accompanied by the British War Medal and Victory Medal.

The 1914/15 Star, authorized in 1918, was awarded for service in France and Belgium after 22 November 1914 and until 31 December 1915, and in all other operational theatres around the world from 5 August 1914 and until 31 December 1915. The 1914/15 Star was not awarded to those personnel who had already qualified for the 1914 Star. As with the 1914 Star, the 1914/15 Star should always be accompanied by a British War Medal and a Victory Medal.

The British War Medal 1914–20 (BWM) was sanctioned in 1919. Qualification for the medal varied slightly depending upon which service the individual was in. Men of the Army, including the RFC, had to have entered a theatre of war or rendered approved service overseas between 5 August 1914 and 11 November 1918. Service in Russia in 1919 and 1920 also qualified for the award.

The Victory Medal (VM), also authorized in 1919, was awarded to those personnel who served on the establishment of a unit in an operational theatre. This medal could not be awarded alone but must always be accompanied by the British War Medal.

The Territorial Force War Medal 1914–19 (TFWM) was awarded to members or former members of the Territorial Force only. To qualify for the award an individual had to have been a member of the Territorial Force on or prior to 30 September 1914, and to have served in an operational theatre outside the United Kingdom between 5 August 1914 and 11 November 1918. Those men who qualified for either the 1914 or 1914/15 Star could not receive this medal.

The Mercantile Marine War Medal 1914–18 was issued by the Board of Trade to personnel of the Merchant Navy who sailed on at least one voyage through a danger area.

The Silver War Badge (SWB), authorized in September 1916, was given to all military personnel who were discharged because of sickness or wounds contracted or received as a result of war service, either at home or overseas at any time after 4 August 1914. The majority of Silver War Badge rolls in WO 329 are for men discharged from the RFC.

The following table gives the National Archives references for those medal rolls that specifically concern the RFC and RAF:

Reference	Medal roll
WO 329/2504	1914 Star RFC other ranks
WO 329/2512	1914 Star RFC officers
WO 329/2926–30	1914/15 Star RFC other ranks
WO 329/2135	BWM and VM RFC other ranks
WO 329/2136–7	BWM and VM RAF other ranks
WO 329/3270	TFWM RFC/RAF
WO 329/3244	SWB RFC

10.2.2 *Using First World War medal rolls (WO 329)*

To search the medal rolls in WO 329, it is necessary to consult the Medal Index Cards (MIC) in the series WO 372 first. These cards are on microfiche and are held in the Open Reading Room. These records have also been digitized and placed on DocumentsOnline. To use these records on microfiche and online require two different approaches.

WO 372 is an alphabetical list of those individuals who qualified for any of the following campaign medals: 1914 Star, 1914/15 Star, British War Medal 1914–20, Victory Medal 1914–19, Territorial Force War Medal 1914–19 and/or were awarded a Silver War Badge.

The MICs are in alphabetical sequence and Regimental Order of Precedence. Names of individuals are usually listed in the following format:

Jones J.
Jones James
Jones John
Jones Julius
Jones James A.
Jones John A.
Jones Julius A.
Jones James B.
Jones John B.

Jones Julius B.
Jones James A.B.
Jones John A.B.

This sequence of surname, followed by single initial, followed by single forename, followed by forename and initial(s), is used throughout the MICs. Each sequence of names is also listed in Regimental Order of Precedence, whereby those men who served in the most senior regiment in the Army appear first and men from the second most senior and subsequent regiments appear in a specific order (see Appendix 6).

On each MIC the following information is given: surname, first forename, name or initial and subsequent initials, rank, regiment, service number, the medals to which the individual was entitled and the Army Medal Office medal roll references for these medals, the name or number of the first operational theatre in which the individual first served, and the date when the individual first entered that theatre. Usually the name of the theatre is given in full, but in some cases just a number and/or letter is given. There were 26 different operational theatres, details of which can be found in 10.2.3. The Army Medal Office references usually appear in the form of an alpha-numeric code, the last part of which is the page number on which the name of the individual appears.

The MICs were filmed onto sheets of microfiche and each sheet contains 360 MICs. When the MICs were filmed they were laid out in a specific pattern.

In order to obtain the correct WO 329 references for the medal rolls and Silver War Badge roll, the sequence to use is as follows:

- Find the sheet of microfiche which includes the surname of the individual you are interested in.
- Find the name of the individual on the MIC.
- Write down the details of Army Medal Office reference numbers, which are noted alongside the names of the medals an individual was awarded.
- Change the Army Medal Office references into WO 329 references using the WO 329/1 key, which is available in the Microfilm Reading Room, as a copied bound volume.
- Order the WO 329 volume you require on one of the computer terminals in the Open Reading Room.

It is possible to obtain photocopies of both the MICs and the medal rolls. Please speak to the staff in the Open Reading Room.

The Medal Index Cards on DocumentsOnline can be searched by name, rank, number and regiment or corps (unit). Unlike the MICs on microfiche, where you may have to search more than one sheet of microfiche for an individual and to understand the Regimental Order of Precedence, searching for an MIC online is in most cases, much easier. There are however, a few tips worth noting.

If an individual has more than one Christian name, you may find that his first name is given in full and the second name is given as an initial only. Variations in spelling can cause problems when searching online, so you may wish to search using a shortened name and ending it with *. It is also possible to use an * with a regimental number if you are unsure of the ending, or a regiment or corps title if you are unsure how they were recorded on an MIC. Examples of regimental titles include Devon or Devonshire, so searching with devon* will pick up both. A man who served in the artillery may have served in the Royal Artillery, Royal Horse Artillery or even the Royal Garrison Artillery. Searching using artillery only will pick them all up.

10.2.3 *Operational theatres of war 1914–20*
The alpha-numeric codes for each theatre of war, e.g. 1a, relating to service in France and Belgium in the Western European theatre of war, are also used in the service records. For those men who first saw operational service before 31 December 1915 and therefore received a 1914 Star or 1914/15 Star as well as the British War and Victory Medals, the numerical codes used differ slightly from those used for men who only saw their first operational service from 1 January 1916 onwards.

Pre-31/12/1915	Post-1/1/1916	
1	1	WESTERN EUROPE
		a France and Belgium
		b Italy
2	2	BALKANS
		a Greek Macedonia, Serbia, Bulgaria and European Turkey
		b Gallipoli (Dardanelles)
	3	RUSSIA (4/5 August 1914–1/2 July 1920)
3	4	EGYPT
		a 4/5 November 1914–18/19 March 1916
		b 18/19 March 1916–31 October/1 November 1918
4	5	AFRICA
		a East Africa, Nyasaland and Northern Rhodesia
		b South West Africa
		c Cameroon
		d Nigeria
		e Togoland

5   6 ASIA

                a Hejaz

                b Mesopotamia

                c Persia

                d Trans Caspia

                e South West Arabia

                f Aden

                g Frontier regions of India

                h Tsing-Tau

6   7 AUSTRALASIA

                a New Britain

                b New Ireland

                c Kaiser Wilhelmland

                d Admiralty Islands

                e Nauru

                f German Samoa

For more details relating to these operational theatres, see *The Collector and Researcher's Guide to the Great War* by Howard Williamson.

10.2.4 *Other campaigns*

The only other campaign medal which men of the RFC won was the Khedive's Sudan Medal 1910, the roll of which is in WO 100/407.

10.3 Royal Naval Air Service: Campaign Medals

The First World War campaign medal rolls for members of the RNAS can be found in ADM 171. ADM 171/89–91 contains the medal roll for officers and ADM 171/94–119 contains the medal roll for RN ratings. The roll for men of the Royal Marines can be found in ADM 171/167–71. In many cases, although the name of an individual may be found in the medal rolls, the entry says that the medal(s) may have been issued by the Air Ministry (AM). Although there are no Air Ministry Medal Rolls, details regarding what medal(s) a man received can be found on his record of service. See chapter 6 for further details.

All of the First World War medal rolls are arranged in alphabetical order. The entry can provide surname, first name and initial, service number, rank, which medal(s) the individual was entitled to (abbreviated to 14ST for 1914 Star, C meaning clasp for the 1914 Star, ST for 1914/15 Star, B for British War Medal and V for Victory Medal) and how the medals were disposed of (where they were sent).

A separate roll for the 1914 Star awarded to naval personnel can be found in ADM 171/139. The Silver War Badge rolls for men of the RNAS are amongst the RN Silver War Badge rolls in ADM 171/173–87. These rolls are arranged by applications, which are by name and either officer or rating, or by badge number.

ADM 171/173	Officers' Applications
ADM 171/175 and 179	Ratings' Applications: A–D
ADM 171/176 and 180	Ratings' Applications: E–K
ADM 171/177 and 181	Rating's Applications: L–M
ADM 171/178 and 182	Ratings' Applications: N–Z
ADM 171/183	Badge numbers 1–10,200
ADM 171/184	Badge numbers 10,201–20,440
ADM 171/185	Badge numbers 20,441–30,580
ADM 171/186	Badge numbers 30,581–45,800
ADM 171/187	Badge numbers 45,801–48,600
	(includes lists of returned badges)

Medal rolls for campaigns involving the Fleet Air Arm are still held by the Naval Medal Office. See Appendix 2 for further details.

10.4   Royal Air Force: Campaign Medals

As such there are no specific First World War campaign medal rolls for the RAF in any AIR record series. All of the data relating to men of the RFC can be found in WO 329 and that of RNAS men in ADM 171.

In many cases men who qualified for at least a 1914 Star or 1914/15 Star serving in any regiment or corps of the Army apart from the RFC, prior to transfer, may have a Medal Index Card (WO 372). Men who qualified for just a British War and Victory Medal whilst serving in any regiment or corps of the British Army apart from the RFC, prior to transfer, may also have a Medal Index Card (WO 372). Men who only saw operational service in the RAF after 1 April 1918 will probably not have a Medal Index Card (WO 372).

The only way to verify the medal entitlement of many men who saw service in the Royal Air Force only during the First World War is to look at their records of service. See chapter 7 for more details.

Apart from the Silver War Badge (SWB) records for the RFC in WO 329, the only true RAF record relating to the SWB can be found in AIR 2/197/C33296.

10.4.1   *Post-1918 campaigns*
Although the RAF has been involved in a number of different operations for which campaign medals were awarded for service since 1918, the

National Archives only has the medal roll for one of these campaigns. Some details relating to post-1918 campaign medals may be found on records of service. See chapter 7.

Operations against the 'Mad Mullah' in Somaliland in January and February 1920, by a number of DH 9as of Z Unit, resulted in the award of the African General Service Medal with the Somaliland 1920 clasp to just over 200 members of the RAF. The medal roll for this award can be found in AIR 2/2267–70. All other post-1918 campaign medal records apart from this exception are still held by the Ministry of Defence. See Appendix 2 for further details.

Applications for Second World War campaign medals and stars for members of civil airlines who carried out flights in operational areas can be found in BT 245/321 and 322.

Applications by civilian members of the RAF Ferry Organization, who flew aircraft from places of manufacture, repair or maintenance or from operational units can be found in AIR 2/11915.

10.5 Awards for Gallantry and Meritorious Service

Beyond medals awarded for just being there are awards for gallantry and meritorious service. Those individuals who performed acts of gallantry or who carried out their normal tasks above the standards normally expected could receive official recognition of such deeds in the form of additional awards.

All awards to British nationals were announced in the *London Gazette* (see 10.9). Many of these announcements were accompanied by citations (a brief explanation relating to the circumstances of the award) and many were not. It is the surviving recommendations for the honours and awards which you need to find in order to discover the story behind these awards.

Awards to foreign nationals who served in the RFC and RAF did not usually appear in the *London Gazette* and consequently the recommendation for the award should be sought. There are plenty of files in AIR 2 concerning awards to these men.

10.5.1 *Royal Engineers Balloon Section*
Prior to the First World War, and indeed the formation of the RFC, only a small number of officers and only two men (Sgt W.H. Pearce and Sgt W.J. Wellman, both of No.1 Balloon Section, who received the Distinguished Conduct Medal [*London Gazette*, 26 June 1902]) of the RE Balloon Section were decorated for services in the Boer War. Records relating to the deeds for which these men were decorated are not easily found. Apart

from looking at the Royal Engineers' history, a copy of which is available in the National Archives Library, the only likely record sources available are the South African War papers in WO 108, War Office Registered Papers: General Series in WO 32 Code 'O' AU and Code 50, Submissions for the Distinguished Conduct Medal in WO 146 and the announcements which appear in the *London Gazette* in ZJ 1.

10.5.2 *Royal Flying Corps*

The most important thing to remember when researching gallantry and meritorious awards won by members of the RFC is that the RFC was a corps of the British Army. Therefore any awards won by men of the RFC prior to April 1918 are likely to be Army awards.

The Victoria Cross (VC) (which could be awarded to both officers and other ranks) was and still is the highest award for gallantry in the face of the enemy. Prior to the creation of the RAF's own specific awards in 1918 the Distinguished Service Order (DSO) and the Military Cross (MC) were the only other awards available to recognize acts of gallantry by officers.

The register of the Victoria Cross is in the series WO 98 and these registers have been digitized and placed on DocumentsOnline where they can be searched by name.

For other ranks, apart from the VC, the only other awards available to recognize acts of gallantry were the Distinguished Conduct Medal (DCM) and, from 1916, the Military Medal (MM).

Due to the complex nature of the statutes of the DSO, MC, DCM and MM, it was in fact possible for them also to be awarded for distinguished service, as well as just for gallantry in the face of the enemy.

From 1916 the Meritorious Service Medal (MSM) was awarded to a number of men for gallantry, not in the face of the enemy, but primarily for good service above that normally expected. Lists of names of men awarded the MSM were published in the *London Gazette*.

The lowest form of official recognition was a Mentioned in Despatches (MiD). Although a recipient did not receive a separate medal for this, he was entitled to wear a bronze oakleaf on the Victory Medal ribbon, signifying that he had been Mentioned in Despatches. Recipients of an MiD also received a certificate giving the name of the recipient, whose despatch they were mentioned in, and the date on which their name was published in the *London Gazette*.

All awards for gallantry and meritorious service were announced in the official state newspaper, the *London Gazette*. Many of the announcements were accompanied by brief citations describing the deed for which the award was granted. See 10.9 on how to use the *London Gazette*.

Fuller descriptions of the deeds for which honours and awards were granted may be found in files concerning recommendations for such awards. The majority of surviving recommendations for honours and awards are in the record series AIR 1. There are no general sections within AIR 1 where these files may be found. They are distributed throughout the whole series. To find many of these files it helps if you know which squadron or wing an individual was serving in at the time of the award, as this can help you limit the number of files you need to look at. A few of the files which contain recommendations for honours and awards are listed below.

AIR 1/993/204/5/1216	Recommendations for honours and awards, RFC in the field, August–October 1916
AIR 1/1479/204/36/131	New Year's honours *Gazette* correspondence, September 1917–February 1919
AIR 1/1522/204/67/19	Honours and awards, December 1917–May 1918
AIR 1/1526/204/68/19	Honours and awards, June 1917–January 1919
AIR 1/2147/209/3/131	Recommendations for honours and awards, HQ RFC France, October 1915

You can look for honours and award files in AIR 1 using two methods:

1 Do a keyword search on the Catalogue, using such search terms as honour(s), award(s), recommendation, decoration(s) and the squadron number if you know it.

2 Search the AIR 1 card index, available in the Open Reading Room, using similar terms to those listed above. The card index will provide you with the original Air Historical Branch (AHB) reference for a file, which can then be used with the AIR 1 series list to identify the full TNA document reference.

Other record sources concerning honours and awards include:

WO 389	The DSO and MC Gazette Book, which includes citations similar to those which appear in the *London Gazette*, many of which are annotated with further details
WO 390	Register of the DSO
WO 391	Register of the DCM
WO 388	Register of Foreign Awards.

All of these records are available on microfilm in the Open Reading Room.

Card indexes listing those men who were awarded the DCM, MM or MSM are available in the Open Reading Room. Each index provides name, rank, service number and unit details, and notes the date on which the award was announced in the *London Gazette*. WO 389/9–24 contains an alphabetical list of all those commissioned and warrant officers awarded the Military Cross (MC). Each entry provides name, rank, unit and *London Gazette* date.

The National Archives Library has a large number of books concerning honours and awards and those who received them. All of the most important books about honours and awards are listed under Further Reading, including the DFC roll, DFM roll and the DSO 1886–1923.

10.5.3 Royal Naval Air Service

As the Royal Naval Air Service was administered by the Admiralty, its members were awarded naval gallantry awards.

As already mentioned, the ultimate reward for gallantry was, and still is, the Victoria Cross. Only two members of the RNAS were awarded the VC. Flight Lieutenant Rex Warneford was awarded the VC for destroying the German zeppelin LZ37 on 7 June 1915, the award being gazetted on 11 June of the same year. Squadron Commander, later Vice Admiral, Richard Bell-Davies was awarded the VC for rescuing a colleague who had been shot down near Ferejik Junction, Bulgaria, on 19 November 1915, the award being announced in the *London Gazette* on 1 January 1916. Bell-Davies's flight report for this incident can be found in AIR 1/649/17/122/421.

Naval aviators and others serving in the RNAS were eligible for a number of different awards, including the Distinguished Service Order (DSO), Distinguished Service Cross (DSC), Conspicuous Gallantry Medal (CGM) and Distinguished Service Medal (DSM). A Naval Meritorious Service Medal (MSM) was instituted in January 1919, with many retrospective awards being made for service in the First World War.

Much as with the RFC, there are a number of different record series containing details concerning honours and awards granted to members of the RNAS.

The most important record collection relating to honours and awards granted to officers and warrant officers of the RNAS is the collection of 'Honours Sheets' in ADM 171. These sheets contain much detail that does not appear in the *London Gazette*. The 'Honours Sheets' are in ADM 171/78–88 and are arranged by sheet identification letter and page number. A nominal card index providing sheet and page number of those who appear within the sheets is available in the Document Reading Room.

Beyond the 'Honours Sheets' there are a number of other record series of both the Admiralty and Air Ministry where further files concerning honours and awards may be found.

Admiralty correspondence in ADM 1, ADM 116 and ADM 137 contains files relating to honours and awards. These three record classes can all be searched using the Admiralty Index and Digest in ADM 12. Searches of ADM 12 can be made either for the individual using the alphabetical indexes or by using the numerical 'Digest' code indexes. The 'Digest' codes worth using are 85a Honours and Rewards or 90 Aviation. Apart from 1914, there are two volumes of ADM 12 for each part of the alphabet or range of 'Digest' numbers for the period 1915–19, each of which needs to be searched. A 'How to Use ADM 12' leaflet is available upon request from the desk in the Open Reading Room.

Once again a keyword search on the computerized Catalogue may provide some references. See Using the National Archives (see p. 7) for further information.

The only piece of ADM 116 which relates specifically to RNAS honours and awards is ADM 116/1560 Honours and Awards for service during the period ending 31 December 1917.

As the RNAS combined with the RFC to form the RAF, a large number of files concerning RNAS honours and awards are also to be found in AIR 1. See 10.5.2 Royal Flying Corps for information about using AIR 1. These files include, for example, AIR 1/75/15/9/173, RNAS Dunkerque Command – Honours and awards gained by officers and men, 1916–19.

All awards for gallantry or meritorious service were announced in the *London Gazette*, with citations accompanying many awards. For information about the *London Gazette*, see 10.9.

A number of very useful books concerning the DSC and DSM are available for consultation at the National Archives. *Fringes of the Fleet* by Richard Witte about the DSC and *The Distinguished Service Medal 1914–1920* by W.H. Fevyer both contain useful information.

Rolls of the CGM, DSM and Naval MSM can be found in ADM 171/61. A roll of the CGM and DSM is in ADM 171/75. A roll of the CGM can also be found in ADM 1/25295.

A roll of foreign orders awarded to naval officers can be found in ADM 171/67.

Names of naval officers submitted for appointment to the Order of the British Empire can be found in ADM 171/135–7.

10.6 Royal Air Force Awards

10.6.1 *First World War*

The creation of the RAF on 1 April 1918 brought with it the need for new honours and awards for the new service. The Distinguished Flying Cross, Air Force Cross, Distinguished Flying Medal and Air Force Medal were all instituted in June 1918. Details of these can be found in AIR 2/59 and ADM 1/8511/15. Thus, before the end of the war it would be possible to see officers and men of the RAF wearing Army and RAF honours and Navy and RAF honours.

Sources concerning awards granted to officers and men of the RAF can

Fig. 34 (facing)
*An illustration of
the device used in
the famous 'Wooden
Horse' escape from
a German POW camp
in WW2.* WO 373/95

be found in AIR 1, within the units' records and in AIR 30, Submissions to the Sovereign. Although the majority of recommendations for awards are in AIR 1, a number of files may also be found in AIR 2, Series A, Code 32/1 and AIR 2, Series B, Code 30.

Amongst the records in AIR 1 are:

RAF Honours and awards
  August 1918–April 1919   AIR 1/107/15/9/287
Record of Honours awarded: Unit index book
  July–November 1918   AIR 1/878/204/5/584

10.6.2 Inter-war years

Between 1919 and 1939 officers and men of the Royal Air Force were decorated for their gallantry not only in operational flying but also for numerous pioneering flights around the world. Files can be found in AIR 2, Series A, Codes 32/1 and 32/2, AIR 2, Series B, Code 30, AIR 5 and AIR 8.

The majority of surviving recommendations for awards for gallantry in operations can be found amongst the records relating to those operations. See 8.5 for further details. Recommendations for awards for operations in Somaliland in 1920 can be found in AIR 2/204. Files containing recommendations for long distance flights in 1919 and 1920 can be found in AIR 2/110 and AIR 2/119. Recommendations for awards to the crew of the airship R33 in 1925 can be found in AIR 2/277.

Bravery awards connected with the R101 airship disaster are recorded in AIR 2/8783.

The long-distance flights from Egypt to Australia were recognized with awards, details of which can be found in AIR 2/4022.

Awards for service in Mesopotamia (later Iraq) between 1918 and 1920 can be found in AIR 2/2841. A file concerning awards for services in the Penjwin area of Iraq in 1927 can be found in AIR 5/222.

Operational awards for service in Waziristan in 1937 and 1938 can be found in AIR 2/2516, 3803, 9393 and 9404. Awards for service in Palestine immediately prior to the Second World War can be found in AIR 2/9404.

Citations for a number of operational awards were published in the *London Gazette*. See 10.9 for further details.

Submissions to the Sovereign in AIR 30 also contain some brief details relating to awards granted between the wars.

10.6.3 Second World War

Owing to the changing nature of warfare in the Second World War, it is not surprising to find that one of the most common gallantry awards between 1939 and 1945 was for gallantry in the air: the Distinguished Flying Cross (DFC), of which over 20,000 were awarded.

The majority of files containing recommendations for awards granted

Rough Sketch of the Horse.

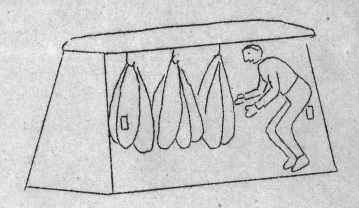

"X-Ray" view of the horse being brought in with worker and 12 full sandbags.   The four bearers and removable carrying poles have been omitted.

The Horse is taken in after vaulting.

to RAF personnel in the Second World War are in AIR 2, Series B, Code 30, AIR 2 Numerical Lists and some in WO 373, most notably WO 373/47 and 105. Records in the series WO 373 have been digitized and placed on DocumentsOnline, where it is possible to search for individual awards by name.

In order to research any Second World War RAF award for gallantry or meritorious service it helps to know when the award was announced in the *London Gazette*. The best source to start your research with is *Honour the Air Forces* by M. Maton, as this book lists all awards and their gazette dates. However, the book does not list MiDs.

There were different categories as well as types of awards bestowed upon men and women of the RAF and WRAF. Awards for flying were split into both operational and non-operational, and also into immediate awards (those requiring recognition of a specific act or acts within a short period) or non-immediate awards (recognizing courage over a longer given period, usually a tour of operations). Gallant acts on the ground, rescuing aircrew from crashed aircraft, for example, were also recognized, as were acts of meritorious service in support of operations.

Files relating to flying awards granted to personnel of the Army and Navy who served with the RAF may also be found in AIR 2. The RAF also controlled the committee which oversaw the award of the George Cross (GC), George Medal (GM) and the British Empire Medal (BEM). Consequently it is possible to find these awards made to soldiers and sailors as well as airmen.

Numerous awards were granted for some of the most famous air operations between 1939 and 1945. Awards for the Battle of Britain can be found in AIR 2/4086, 4095, 8351 and 9468. The recommendation for the only Victoria Cross won during the battle can be found in AIR 2/5686.

As there are so many files relating to awards granted between 1939 and 1946 it is again useful to know when the award was announced in the *London Gazette* and/or the original Air Ministry file reference containing the recommendation.

10.6.4 Nominal indexes of RAF awards

There are several hundred files concerning honours and awards granted for services in the Second World War. Unless you have certain details which can help you narrow your search, you may have to look at a number of different files before you find the information you seek. You may be able to find the details you need in two indexes containing information which can enable a researcher to find the correct AIR 2 file. The Honours section at RAF Innsworth has a nominal index which can provide the reference to the Air Ministry file in which details relating to a given award were originally placed. Many of these files no longer exist and only the National

Fig. 35 (facing) *A very rare post 1970 RAF recommendation for an award.* DEFE 71/52

HONOURS - IN CONFIDENCE

RESTRICTED

CITATION

(To be completed by Initiating Officer)

Army Form W 3121
(Revised)

A. Recommended in respect of:—

    (i) ~~New Year Battle~~

    (ii) ~~Birthday Battle~~

    (iii) ~~Immediate Award (operational)~~

    (iv) Operational Award (other than immediate)

    (v) ~~Non-operational Gallantry Award~~

    (vi) ~~Meritorious Service Medal~~

} Delete all descriptions not applicable.

B. Action or service for which commended:—

    (i) Place .... Northern Ireland ....

    *(ii) Date of action or period covered by the citation .... 15th April 1976 ....

    (iii) How employed .... Pilot ....

    (iv) Other detail:—

At 1945 hours on 15th April 1976 a Royal Air Force Wessex helicopter in support of the Army, was severely damaged by a RPG 7 missile and groundfire as it approached the Security Forces Helicopter Landing Site at Crossmaglen in South Armagh.   The Royal Air Force Support Helicopter Detachment Commander, who was at the Battalion Headquarters at Bessbrook some 11 miles to the north-east at the time of the incident, immediately took charge of the situation and accompanied a number of technicians to Crossmaglen to undertake a detailed inspection of the damaged aircraft.   The situation at Crossmaglen was tense. A fierce gun battle had taken place between Security Forces and terrorists in which some 500 rounds had been exchanged; it was dark and the aircraft was vulnerable to further attack.   ▆▆▆▆▆▆▆▆▆ quickly appraised the situation and knowing that the ground inspection might not have revealed all the damage, nevertheless decided to fly the aircraft to the more secure Landing Site at Bessbrook thereby reducing the risk of further attack on the Security Base and his own groundcrew.   ▆▆▆▆▆'s decision was courageous but based on clear thought and good judgement. He asked for and obtained the willing support of the second pilot and crewman to accompany him. He lifted out of Crossmaglen at night on both engines but because of damage to the fuel system, he had to close one engine down at 1500 feet before continuing the flight to Bessbrook where he made a safe landing.   Temporary repairs were carried out at Bessbrook and the aircraft was flown back to Royal Air Force Aldergrove, again by ▆▆▆▆▆▆▆▆▆▆▆, on 19th April 1976.   ▆▆▆▆▆ ▆▆▆▆▆▆▆▆ instantly rose to the difficult situation which presented itself at Crossmaglen: his brave decision made in the knowledge that his personal safety was at considerable risk, was a magnificent example of leadership and devotion to duty.   As a result of this commendable action not only was the risk of further attack on a damaged aircraft averted, but also the Provisional IRA were deprived of the considerable prestige which they would have accrued from their sympathizers had they been able to claim the destruction of a Security Forces Helicopter.   ▆▆▆▆▆▆▆▆▆▆'s leadership and considerable skill resulting from the incident at Crossmaglen are in accord with the finest traditions of the Royal Air Force and deserving of lasting recognition.   I have no hesitation therefore in strongly recommending him for the award of the Distinguished Flying Cross.

A. 1970 hrs   B. 50mins   C. 110 hrs   D. Wessex.

* The period covered by the citation *must* be completed as accurately as possible.

(950046)910143 5/72 31m HPG

RESTRICTED

HONOURS - IN CONFIDENCE

Archives records what survives. The original Air Ministry file reference still needs to be converted into a National Archives document reference, so that the file can be ordered on the computer. Only original recipients or their next of kin will be provided with details by RAF Innsworth (see Appendix 2).

The second nominal index has been compiled over many years by recording all of the names of individuals who appear in the *surviving* AIR 2, Series B, Code 30 honours files, and then putting them into a computer. Many awards were down-graded; many recommendations were unsuccessful. Many individuals were recommended for honours more than once and the computerized index covers all these entries. All awards for gallantry and meritorious service, from the Victoria Cross to Mentioned in Despatches, from Knight Commander of the Order of the Bath to the British Empire Medal, are listed, as are awards to foreign nationals and awards from foreign states to British nationals. For further details about this index contact Paul Baillie, via email paulbaillie@tiscali.co.uk. Paul Baillie also has an index of naval awards, the recommendations for which are in the series ADM 1, ADM 116 and ADM 199.

10.6.5   *Since 1945*

Awards granted to members of the RAF after 1945 continued to be announced in the *London Gazette*, as they still are today. The surviving files containing recommendations for awards are primarily to be found in AIR 2, Series B, Code 30 and the AIR 2 'Numerical List'. It is also possible to identify surviving files by using the Catalogue.

Of the surviving post-war files a number are worth noting:

Reference	Operation
AIR 2/9986	Berlin Airlift
AIR 2/16814	Recommendations for Malaya, June 1950 onwards
AIR 2/16185	Recommendations for Korea, December 1950 onwards
AIR 2/12276	US awards to RAF personnel in Korea, 1951
AIR 2/12423	Kenya, 1953–5
AIR 2/12424	Kenya, 1955–6
AIR 8/2125	Operation Musketeer, Suez, 1956
AIR 2/17390	Operations in South Arabia, 1964
AIR 2/17385	Ground Gallantry Awards April 1964–July 1965
AIR 2/17386	Flying Awards April 1964–December 1965
AIR 2/17487	Ground Gallantry Awards August 1965–February 1968
AIR 2/17489	New Year Awards 1966: Flying Awards
AIR 2/17532	Flying Awards: Recommended January 1966–February 1968
AIR 2/18214	Birthday Honours: Flying Awards 1968
AIR 2/18257	Ground Gallantry Awards 1968–71
AIR 2/18258	Flying Gallantry Awards 1967–70
AIR 2/18268	New Year Awards 1969: Flying Awards

Apart from the Honours and Awards records in AIR 2, it may also be possible to find more recent RAF award files in DEFE 71.

10.7 Fleet Air Arm Awards

10.7.1 Second World War

Surviving recommendations for honours and awards to members of the Fleet Air Arm can be found in a number of different record series. The series containing the most is ADM 1, Series 1, Code 85, with further awards within the same series under ADM 1, Series 2, Code 85 and ADM 1 'Numerical List'. With the advent of online keyword searches, it is possible to find the necessary files, as long as you know the name of the ship, squadron or operation. As with the award files in AIR 2, not all of the Admiralty award files have survived.

It helps when looking for an award for gallantry or meritorious service to know when the award was announced in the *London Gazette* and any other details such as operation, squadron or ship. *Seedies Roll of Naval Awards 1939–1959* can provide the key data to use when researching awards.

When a number of files relating to a specific subject were compiled, they were sometimes turned into case files. These case files can be found in ADM 116, and the relevant files relating to awards can be found in ADM 116, Code 85. A small number of files concerning awards can also be found in the operational records in ADM 199. The recommendation for the award of a posthumous Victoria Cross to Temp. Lt R.H. Gray RCNVR can be found in ADM 1/24300. Amongst other honours and awards (H&A) files in Admiralty record series are:

ADM 1/11260	Awards for the sinking of the *Bismarck*
ADM 1/12459 and 12460	Awards for attacks on German warships *Scharnhorst*, *Gneisenau* and *Prinz Eugen*
ADM 1/16695	Awards to personnel of aircraft carriers *Formidable*, *Furious* and *Indefatigable* for air attacks on the *Tirpitz*
ADM 116/5648	Report on the Fleet Air Arm attack on the *Tirpitz* and recommendations for awards

10.7.2 Since 1945

Although personnel of the Fleet Air Arm have been involved in numerous operations around the world since 1945, the number of files containing the recommendations for awards is very small. Surviving honours and awards files for the post-1945 period can be found in ADM 1, Series 2, Code 85, ADM 1 'Numerical List' and ADM 116, Code 85. With the advent of online searching of the Catalogue locating possible files should be easier.

10.8   Glider Pilot Regiment and Army Air Corps Awards

The nature of the job men of the GPR and AAC performed was such that they might receive gallantry awards for service both in the air and on the ground. As this is the case it is possible to find recommendations for awards in AIR 2, Series B, Code 30 and in WO 373. The majority of awards for gallantry whilst flying are in AIR 2, and those for gallantry on the ground are in WO 373. Apart from a specific policy file concerning the process by which men of the GPR could be recommended for flying awards, the recommendations for awards are distributed amongst the award files in AIR 2. A full list of the awards gained by men of the GPR can be found in *The History of the Glider Pilot Regiment* by Claude Smith.

Due to the nature of Army flying, a member of the GPR or AAC could receive an award for flying service or ground service. It may be necessary to look in more than one place. To assist your research you may wish to consult *Honour the Armies* by M. Maton as this contains an alphabetical listing of all Army awards and their gazette dates. The book unfortunately does not include MiDs.

Of the awards for post-1945 operations, flying awards to Army personnel for service in Korea can be found in WO 373/119 and similar awards for service in Malaya 1951–60 can be found in WO 373/136.

10.9   The *London Gazette*

The *London Gazette*, founded in 1665, is the official government newspaper containing acts of state, proclamations and appointments to offices under the crown. All military appointments and announcements relating to commissions into the armed forces, promotions and announcements relating to awards for gallantry and meritorious service or Mentioned in Despatches are published in the *London Gazette*. The paper is published periodically throughout each month of the year. The page numbering is sequential from the beginning of the year to the end. At the end of each quarter (March, June, September and December), half year (June and December) or end of year (December), indexes are published which list the various subjects and names of individuals that have appeared in the paper during a given period.

The *London Gazette* is available at the National Archives in three different formats. The whole paper can be found in the series ZJ 1. The volumes for the First World War and Second World War are also available on microfilm in the Open Reading Room. Finally the papers are also available online.

Index volumes for the periods 1914–21 and 1940–6 are available in the

Open Reading Room. Each year of these indexes is split into quarters. All other indexes need to be identified in the *London Gazette* (ZJ 1) series list and ordered on the computer.

In order to find the particular entry for an individual, you need to have certain information that will enable you to find the correct edition. It will help if you have any of the following: name, rank and unit, type of award and the approximate date.

Prior to 1942, each section of a *London Gazette* index concerning honours and awards was arranged in alphabetical order by name of award, and then the list of names of recipients in alphabetical order, each name with a page number. After 1941, rather than be split into various sections representing each different honour, the *London Gazette* indexes were split into sections headed: Honours and Distinctions; Mentioned in Despatches; and Commendations.

As each index represents a given part of the year, for example, a quarter, the page number relating to an individual will appear within that period. Once you have identified the page number where an announcement is located, apply the page number to the *London Gazette* (ZJ 1) class list and order that volume of the *London Gazette* which has the page number in it.

The *London Gazette* is accessible via its own website *www.gazettes-online.co.uk*. It is possible to search the whole of the *London Gazette* from its inception right up to date.

10.10 Long Service Awards

Long service and good conduct medals (LSGCs) were and still are awarded to military personnel with an unblemished career over a given period. This period varied according to the service into which an individual entered. The various types of awards issued by different services are described below.

10.10.1 *Army issue*
The LSGC awarded to members of the RE Balloon Section, 37 members of the RFC and 8 members of the RAF, was awarded for 18 years' unblemished service. The medal rolls for the army issue LSGC can be found in WO 102. With the creation of the RAF in 1918, members of the RAF became eligible for their own award – see 10.10.3.

10.10.2 *Royal Navy issue*
Men of the RNAS and Fleet Air Arm had to have served for at least 15 years with unblemished conduct in order to qualify for the LSGC. The

medal rolls for the RN issue LSGC are in ADM 171. Only ADM 171/73 contains the names of men of the RNAS who were awarded the medal. Other LSGC rolls are in ADM 171/140–5 and ADM 171/149–59. As the Fleet Air Arm still exists, this medal is still being issued.

Men of the Fleet Air Arm who served in the Royal Fleet Reserve (RFR) and who went on to qualify for the RFR LSGC may be found in ADM 171/160–3. It is possible to identify Fleet Air Arm RFR personnel as they will have (Lee) in their service number.

10.10.3 Royal Air Force issue

Announced in Air Ministry Weekly Order 520 of 1918 and instituted by Royal Warrant on 1 July 1919, the RAF LSGC was awarded for 18 years served with unblemished conduct. The ribbon of this medal, half crimson and half navy blue, with white edges, represents its Army and Navy counterparts, signifying the origins of the RAF. As the award was made retrospective from 1 April 1918, it was possible for men who had seen initial service in the Army and Navy prior to transfer into the RAF to qualify for this award also. Awards of the RAF LSGC were announced in Air Ministry Weekly Orders (AMWOs) between 1919 and 1941, and between 1950 and 1964. Some AMWOs can be found in AIR 72. The RAF Museum at Hendon has a complete run of AMWOs (see 15.6 for more detail).

Fig. 36 (right) *RAF Long Service and Good Conduct Medal, obverse (left), reverse (right). The obverse has a bar denoting a second award of the same medal.*

Fig. 37 (facing) *An Air Ministry Order announcing a number of RAF Long Service and Good Conduct Medals.* AIR 72/8

ROUTINE ORDER SUPPLEMENT.

239.—Long Service and Good Conduct Medal—Awards.

(537308/24.)

The Long Service and Good Conduct Medal has been awarded to the undermentioned airmen :—

Official number.	Rank.	Name.	With effect from
3450	S.M.1.	Frier, L.	2.3.26
329	S.M.1.	Goddard, F. W.	19.2.26
152	S.M.1.	James, F.	6.1.26
256	S.M.1.	Norman, R. E.	28.1.26
314187	S.M.2.	Elms, W. P.	25.7.20
166040	S.M.2.	Judge, A.	5.8.25
313807	S.M.2.	Lingane, J. P.	1.1.26
185599	S.M.2.	Prax, J. E.	28.1.26
168	S.M.2.	Woolsey, A. L.	28.10.25
314847	F/Sgt.	Burgess, A. C.	26.9.25
337182	F/Sgt.	Clayton, D. C.	29.11.25
314881	F/Sgt.	French, J. W.	20.3.25
2921	F/Sgt.	Hawes, W. M.	19.2.26
338016	Sgt.	Smith, G.	4.12.25
1349	Act. Sgt.	Murton, S. C.	11.12.25
340342	L.A.C.	Williams, C. H.	23.12.25

240.—Long Service and Good Conduct Medal—Award of Certificate to Ex-Naval Ratings.

(608856/25.)

Certificates in accordance with para. 251 of The King's Regulations and Air Council Instructions have been awarded to the undermentioned airmen :—

313704 Flight Sergeant Downs, L.—with effect from 1st January, 1926.

314376 Flight Sergeant Smith, T.—with effect from 1st January, 1926.

241.—Cadets' Inter-Collegiate Athletic Contest.

(685399/26.)

1. A triangular contest (the first of the kind) between the Royal Military Academy, Woolwich, Royal Military College, Sandhurst, and the Royal Air Force Cadet College, Cranwell, will take place at Queen's Club, on Saturday, 8th May, at 3 p.m.

2. The cost of admission to the ground will be one shilling.

A bar signifying a further award of the medal was authorized in 1944. In 1947 the medal was made available to officers promoted from the ranks as long as they had served 12 years in the ranks. In 1977 all three services standardized the length of service an individual other rank needed to serve in order to be awarded an LSGC medal to 15 years.

An example of the George V period RAF LSGC can be seen in Fig. 36.

10.10.4 *The Air Efficiency Award*

The Air Efficiency Award was instituted in September 1942 and was awarded to both officers and men for 10 years' efficient service in the Royal Auxiliary Air Force and Royal Air Force Volunteer Reserve. Officers who received this award were permitted to place the letters AE after their name. A roll of the *Air Efficiency Award 1942–2005* by Chris Brooks was published by the Orders and Medals Research Society in 2006.

The Air Efficiency Award has recently been replaced by the Volunteer Reserves Service Medal (VRSM). Awards of the VRSM are announced in the *London Gazette*.

10.11 Coronation and Jubilee Medals

The medal rolls for the 1911 Coronation Medal for the Army are in the series WO 330/1 and 2 and the Admiralty roll is in ADM 171/61.

The medal rolls for the 1935 Jubilee Medal, 1937 Coronation Medal, 1953 Coronation Medal and the 1977 Jubilee Medal are on the open shelves in the Open Reading Room. These rolls are arranged in alphabetical order and provide name, rank, number and unit.

11 COURTS MARTIAL

As the Royal Air Force was formed from parts of the two other services, it may be necessary to look briefly at the courts martial records created by the Admiralty and War Office, as well as the records created by the Air Ministry and in the case of appeals, the Supreme Court.

Many records of courts martial are closed for up to 100 years. Consequently, although the date of a particular court martial may be known, obtaining more than brief details may be restricted by what is available.

It is possible to search the Catalogue by name of the accused in many of the following records series.

11.1 Admiralty Records

There are really only two Admiralty record series that contain details about courts martial for the period 1908–18, when aviation was in its infancy in the Royal Navy. These series are ADM 1 and ADM 156. If an individual was tried by court martial, there may be an annotation on his record of service (see chapter 6). In order to find any proceedings or further details concerning the case, it may be necessary to consult the alphabetical section of the Admiralty Index and Digest in ADM 12. A brief guide on how to use ADM 12 can be obtained from the Open Reading Room desk.

11.2 War Office Records

War Office courts martial records are many. However, the arrangement of the most important records concerning the RE Balloon Section and RFC means only a small number may need to be consulted, as explained below. The War Office records may also include members of the Army Air Corps and Glider Pilot Regiment.

The Judge Advocate General's (JAG) Office charge books are held in WO 84 and the Registers of Courts Martial are in WO 92 and WO 213.

These records are arranged in chronological order. In the case of WO 213 the date given in the registers is the date when the information was received by the JAG. The trial may have taken place a number of weeks before the information was received in London.

Registers of District Courts Martial between 1829 and 1971 can be found in WO 86. These records are similar to those in WO 213, showing the name, rank and regiment of the accused, together with the place of the trial, charge and sentence.

Similar records to those in WO 86 but concerning courts martial held abroad and covering the period 1779–1960 can be found in WO 90. The same sort of records, but covering India only, between 1878 and 1945, are in WO 88.

Court martial proceedings are in the series WO 71 and can be searched for by name. The majority of First World War records in WO 71 concern those who were tried for military offences that resulted in their execution. WO 71 from 1914 onwards is listed by name and offence and it is possible to search the Catalogue by these parameters. Many of the files in WO 71 that are less than 50 years old are still closed.

11.3   Air Ministry Records

Policy papers relating to courts martial can be found in AIR 2, Series A, Code 21, AIR 2, Series B, Code 28, AIR 2 'Numerical List' and AIR 20, Code 28. The majority of RAF personnel who were tried by court martial were charged or punished under Air Council Instructions (ACI) and King's Regulations (KR RAF) for the RAF. Details of ACI and KR RAF can be found in AIR 10. There are five AIR series that hold JAG Office records dealing specifically with courts martial of RAF personnel:

Reference	Type of record
AIR 18	Proceedings
AIR 21	Registers
AIR 43	Charge books
AIR 44	Minute books
AIR 71	Out-letter books

AIR 18 comprises 134 files and covers the period 1941–94. It contains the proceedings of district, general and field general courts martial of RAF officers and airmen.

AIR 21 comprises 10 volumes and covers the period 1918–65. These registers give name and rank of each prisoner, place of trial, the nature of the offence and the sentence. If an individual was tried by court martial,

Fig. 38,39 (facing and overleaf) *Pages from the proceedings of an RAF Court Martial.* AIR 21/4B

ROYAL AIR FORCE. Form 3.

Order for Assembly and Proceedings of Field General Court-Martial on Active Service.

PROCEEDINGS.

A.

Order convening the court.

On Active Service, this   first   day of   July   , 19 41, .

Whereas it appears to me, the undersigned, an officer in command of RAF Stn, Kalafrana , on active service, that the persons named in the annexed schedule, being subject to the Air Force Act, have committed the offences in the said schedule mentioned ;

And whereas I am of opinion that it is not practicable that such offences should be tried by an ordinary general court-martial *[and that it is not practicable to delay the trial for reference to a superior qualified officer] ;

* Omit where convening officer is a commanding officer, or is of or above the rank of squadron leader.

I hereby convene a field general court-martial to try the said persons, and to consist of the officers hereunder named.

*[I am unable to appoint :—

* Omit if not applicable.

* (1. Three officers to form the court)

* (2. An officer of or above the rank of squadron leader as president)

* (3. Three officers having more than one year's service)

for the following reasons, namely :—

*The ranks, names and units of the President and Members must be inserted before the form is signed by the Convening Officer. The detailing of Members may not be delegated to Officer Commanding units.

*Rank.	President. Name.	Unit.
F/Lt (A/S/Ldr)	P. ALDERTON	RAF Stn, Kalafrana

Rank.	Members. Name.	Unit.
F/Off.(A/F/Lt)	L. AVERY	RAF Stn, Kalafrana.
F/Off.(A/F/Lt)	G.A.V. COLLINS	RAF Stn, Kalafrana.

Judge Advocate.

NIL

* Must be signed personally by the officer actually in command at the time, and all alterations in the composition of the court to be initialled by him.

*Signed *[signature]* Group Captain.

Commanding R.A.F. Station, Kalafrana.

Convening Officer.

(2826-252) Wt. 15801—903 2,000 6/39 T.S. 700
(4026-252) Wt. 37579—3484 12,000 12/39 T.S. 700

"CHARGE SHEET".

The accused, No.524071 Corporal ██████████

Royal Air Force Station, Kalafrana, an airman of the regular

Air Force, is charged with:-

Section 5(5)   When On Active Service.
Air Force Act.

                      By word of mouth, spreading reports
                      calculated to create unnecessary despondency,

                            in that he,

                      at Kalafrana, on the 21st May, 1941, at about
                      1700 hours stated that "the British have allowed
                      the enemy to gain superiority over them, that our
                      patrols have no chance, and that it is sheer
                      murder to send them up and that they should be
                      allowed to use their own initiative whether to
                      attack or not, and not be controlled by people
                      sitting under 30 feet of rock" - or words to the
                      same effect.

                                    [signature]
                                    Group Captain, Commanding,
                                    R.A.F. Station, Kalafrana.

R.A.F. Station, Kalafrana.

23/6/41.

                                                        [signature]
                                                        President.

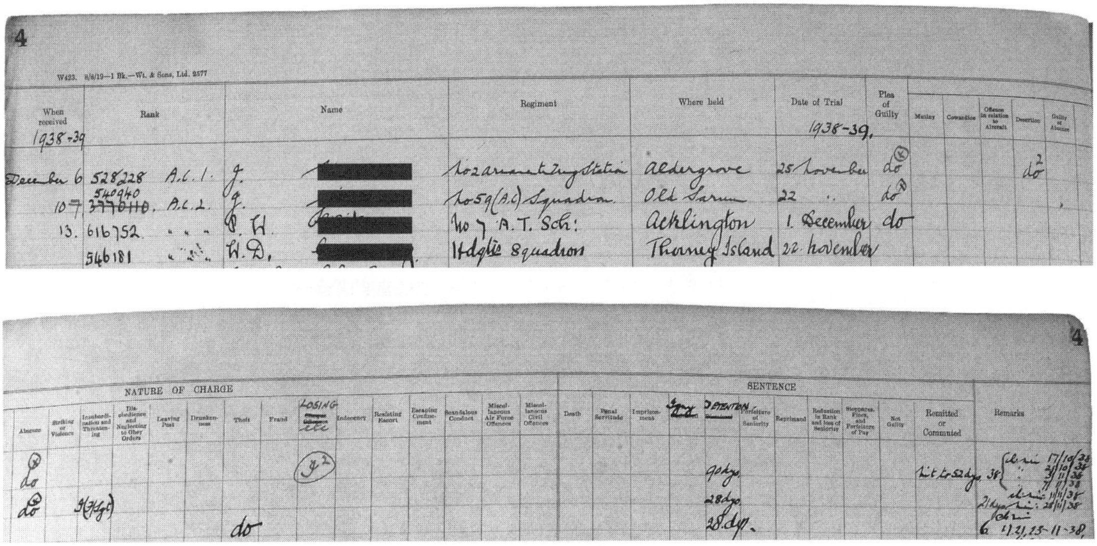

Fig. 40 (above) *Details from facing pages of the RAF registers of Courts Martial.* AIR 18/1

it is to these registers that you should turn first:

The charge books in AIR 43 are very similar to those in WO 213 and are arranged in date order. These charge books provide information on each individual's name, rank, unit, offence, place of trial and the sentence if found guilty.

The minute books in AIR 44 contain details sent to the Judge Advocate General concerning legal aspects, precedents and irregularities, which arose from various RAF courts martial. These records are arranged in chronological order.

The Judge Advocate General's Office Out-Letters in AIR 71 are similar in nature to the records in AIR 43 and AIR 44.

11.4 Supreme Court Records

A number of courts martial cases went to appeal, and these cases were heard by judges in the Supreme Court, rather than any military court. The registers of Courts Martial Appeals can be found in J 152 and the actual cases papers in J 135. These two series cover the period 1952–96 and cover all three armed services.

Fig. 41 *Christmas Card from RNAS, Flanders 1916–17.*
AIR 1/686/21/13/2249

12 PRISONERS OF WAR AND WAR CRIMES

Although members of the British armed forces have been captured in a number of different conflicts, this chapter deals exclusively with those men who fell into enemy hands between 1914 and 1918, and between 1939 and 1945.

12.1 First World War

Records relating to men captured between 1914 and 1918 are scarce. Although the National Archives does not have an exhaustive list of those captured, some details relating to the date and circumstances of capture do survive.

Records of casualties, including those men missing who were subsequently reported as prisoners, can be found amongst the unit operational records in AIR 1. These records include RFC, RNAS and RAF personnel. As far as is known, no records in any Admiralty record class, beyond annotations on records of service, show which members of the RNAS were captured. The total number of members of the RNAS who were captured up to 31 March 1918 was 118 – see AIR 1/109/15/18.

A number of files in WO 161 '1914–1918 War: Miscellaneous Unregistered Papers' contain repatriation reports made by returning prisoners of war after they arrived back in the United Kingdom. The reports in WO 161/95–101 contain details relating to these prisoners' capture, and in many cases mention the names of other individuals who were either captured at the same time or whom the prisoners encountered during their captivity. This collection is only a sample as it does not contain details of all those who had been prisoners of war.

The records in WO 161 have been digitized and placed on DocumentsOnline. It is possible to search by name of individual or by terms such as 'Flying Corps'.

Records of debriefs of escaped airmen can also be found in AIR 1/501/15/233/1.

The Foreign Office had a section responsible for prisoners of war and their records can be found in the series FO 383. The series has been indexed quite effectively, so it is possible to search for individuals by name on the Catalogue.

Officers captured during the First World War had to submit a report on the circumstances of their capture when they were repatriated at the end of the war. Many of these reports survive for officers who served in the various arms of the British Army in the individual's records of service (see chapter 5).

The National Archives does have a published list of officers captured between August 1914 and November 1918. *List of British Officers taken Prisoner in the Various Theatres of War. August 1914–November 1918* is available in the Open Reading Room. The Royal Air Force list, including the RFC, starts on page 146. The RNAS list starts on page 176. The whole work is indexed.

The only other source held by the National Archives which may contain an indication of prisoner of war status is the annotation 'P of W' or 'POW', sometimes found on a Medal Index Card (see chapter 10).

12.2   Second World War

The dominant role of aircraft during the Second World War not surprisingly led to large numbers of men of the flying services falling into enemy hands. Records held by the National Archives relating to prisoners of war captured by the Axis powers are numerous. However, some are not as detailed as others. Many records relating to prisoners of war, prison camps and war crimes can be found in AIR 2 Code 89 and AIR 20 Code 89.

12.2.1   *Lists of prisoners*

There are a number of sources, outlined below, containing basic details of those men, and in some cases women, who were held prisoner at any time between 1939 and 1945.

WO 392 'Prisoner of War lists: Second World War' contains lists of those individuals held by Germany, Italy and Japan. These lists provide name, rank, service number, prisoner number and which camp an individual was held in.

WO 345 'Japanese Index Cards of Allied Prisoners of War and Internees' is arranged in alphabetical order and contains basic biographical and service data, together with dates of capture and the camps in which individuals were imprisoned. Cards that have been crossed through with red lines indicate a prisoner who died in captivity. Further nominal rolls of prisoners held by the Japanese can be found in AIR 49/383–8.

AIR 20/2336 is an alphabetical list of all RAF and Dominion aircrew held by the Germans in 1944–5 and provides service details and where individuals were held.

AIR 40/1488–91 contains nominal rolls of those men held in Stalag Luft III and Stalag IIIA. Stalag Luft III was the camp from which the 'Great Escape' was made in March 1944. Seventy-six officers escaped, of whom fifty who were recaptured were subsequently executed on Hitler's orders – see 12.3.

The National Archives also has a number of published prisoner of war lists available in the Open Reading Room.

12.2.2 Prisoner of war camp records

A number of camp histories can be found in WO 106 'Director of Military Operations and Military Intelligence, and predecessors: Correspondence and Papers', WO 208 'Director of Military Operations and Intelligence and Director of Military Intelligence: Files' and AIR 40 'Directorate of Intelligence'. These histories contain details of some individuals who were imprisoned, but are primarily concerned with details about the camp, its organization and location. AIR 14/461–5 contains details of German camps.

12.2.3 Escaped prisoners of war

A number of men during the Second World War managed either narrowly to evade capture or indeed escape from those holding them. Once again the records relating to these men are not complete, but the records that are available do provide some very interesting details.

The most important collection of records is the MI9 debrief records, completed by escapees and evaders when they returned to the United Kingdom. Many of these records can be found in WO 208 Directorate of Military Intelligence papers, under the references WO 208/3297–3327 and 3348–52. Other examples of these can be found in AIR 14/2072–3 and AIR 40/1533 and 1545–52.

A partial name index of escape and evasion reports for the records in WO 208 can be found in the entrance to the Documents Reading Room. The MI9 references on the cards need to be concerted into WO 208 references.

Two very good studies about men shot down over enemy-occupied territory or into the sea can be found in *Shot Down and On The Run* and *Shot Down and In The Drink*, both by Graham Pitchfork (TNA, 2007).

12.2.4 Repatriated prisoners of war

The most significant collection of records concerning repatriated prisoners of war are the debriefs in WO 344. This series is arranged in two collections; prisoners held by the Germans (and formerly the Italians as appropriate) and prisoners held by the Japanese. Each collection is then arranged in alphabetical order. Each report provides name, rank, number and unit at time of capture. The reports also provide the identity of any camp(s) where the individual was held.

Once again a number of different sources can provide details about airmen captured during the war. AIR 14/469–71 contains reports into the circumstances of capture of RAF aircrew, as do AIR 14/1233 and 1864. Records in WO 208/3328–47 also contain similar information.

A detailed description of RAF POW escape organizations, together with a list of men of the RAF who were captured, can be found in WO 208/3244 and 3245.

12.2.5 Honours and awards

A number of individuals who either escaped or who evaded capture and returned to allied lines were rewarded for their fortitude and gallantry. Many of the MI9 records in WO 208 and AIR 40 are annotated with details relating to the awards these men were given. As their deeds were performed on the ground, it is not surprising to find that these men were awarded either the Military Cross or Military Medal, depending upon rank.

Apart from the annotated records in WO 208 and AIR 40, it is also possible to find recommendations for awards in AIR 2, Series B, Code 30, in files titled 'Ground Gallantry' and also in WO 373, in either the 'Escape and Evasion' section or in the section titled 'The London Omnibus List for Gallant and Distinguished Services in the Field'.

Files concerning men recommended for awards for their actions in POW camps can be found in AIR 40/1488 Stalag Luft III East, AIR 40/1490 Stalag Luft III Belaria, and AIR 40/1491 Stalag IIIA. An example of such a recommendation, that for the award of a Military Cross to Flt Lt O.L.S. Philpot RAF, who was involved in the 'Wooden Horse' escape (see Fig. 34), can be found in WO 373/95 (ff35–ff45).

The World War Two recommendations in WO 373 have been digitized and placed on DocumentsOnline, where it is possible to search by name, rank, service and award. As many RAF personnel received awards for gallantry on the ground, especially when escaping from POW camps or evading capture, it is possible to find details in WO 373 rather than AIR 2.

If you find anything in WO 373 via DocumentsOnline, you can download it for a fee if you are outside the National Archives.

Many foreign nationals assisted escaping and evading RAF personnel and some of them were granted awards by the British government for their help. Recommendations for awards to these 'Helpers' can be found in FO 372 and the records of SOE under the HS departmental code. Keyword search 'helpers' AND 'awards' to obtain further references.

For further details on honours and awards, see chapter 10.

12.3 War Crimes

The execution of 50 of the officers who took part in the 'Great Escape' (see 12.2.1) was not the only instance of a war crime committed against RAF and Dominion personnel during the Second World War.

Records relating to war crimes are distributed amongst a number of different record series. The most useful way to approach this subject is to consult in the Open Reading Room the guide *War Crimes Records in the PRO Originating in the Ministry of Defence: Alphabetical List of Locations etc*. This contains numerous references relating to specific war crimes, their investigation and in some cases the prosecution of the perpetrators.

Documents concerning the 'Great Escape' can be found in AIR 2/10121, AIR 40/266, 268, 270, 285, 287, 2265, 2293, 2313–14 and 2487, WO 32/15502 (Code 91A), WO 208/2901 and 3441, and WO 311/135, 169–82 and 599.

War crimes documents concerning Operation Freshman can be found in WO 309/720, WO 311/383, 386 and 387 and WO 331/16, 17 and 18.

12.4 Missing Personnel

Many service personnel went missing during the Second World War, many on flying operations, many as a result of enemy action at sea. Records relating to enquiries made about missing personnel by all three services are slowly being transferred to the National Archives. The following series have either been transferred and are available or have been assigned to records relating to missing personnel and will be made available in due course.

AIR 81	RAF Personnel. Yet to be transferred
ADM 358	RN Personnel. Yet to be transferred
WO 361	Army Personnel. Available.

Fig. 42 *Pages from a Pilot's Flying Log Book belonging to C.R. Mackenzie. AIR 1/686/21/13/2249*

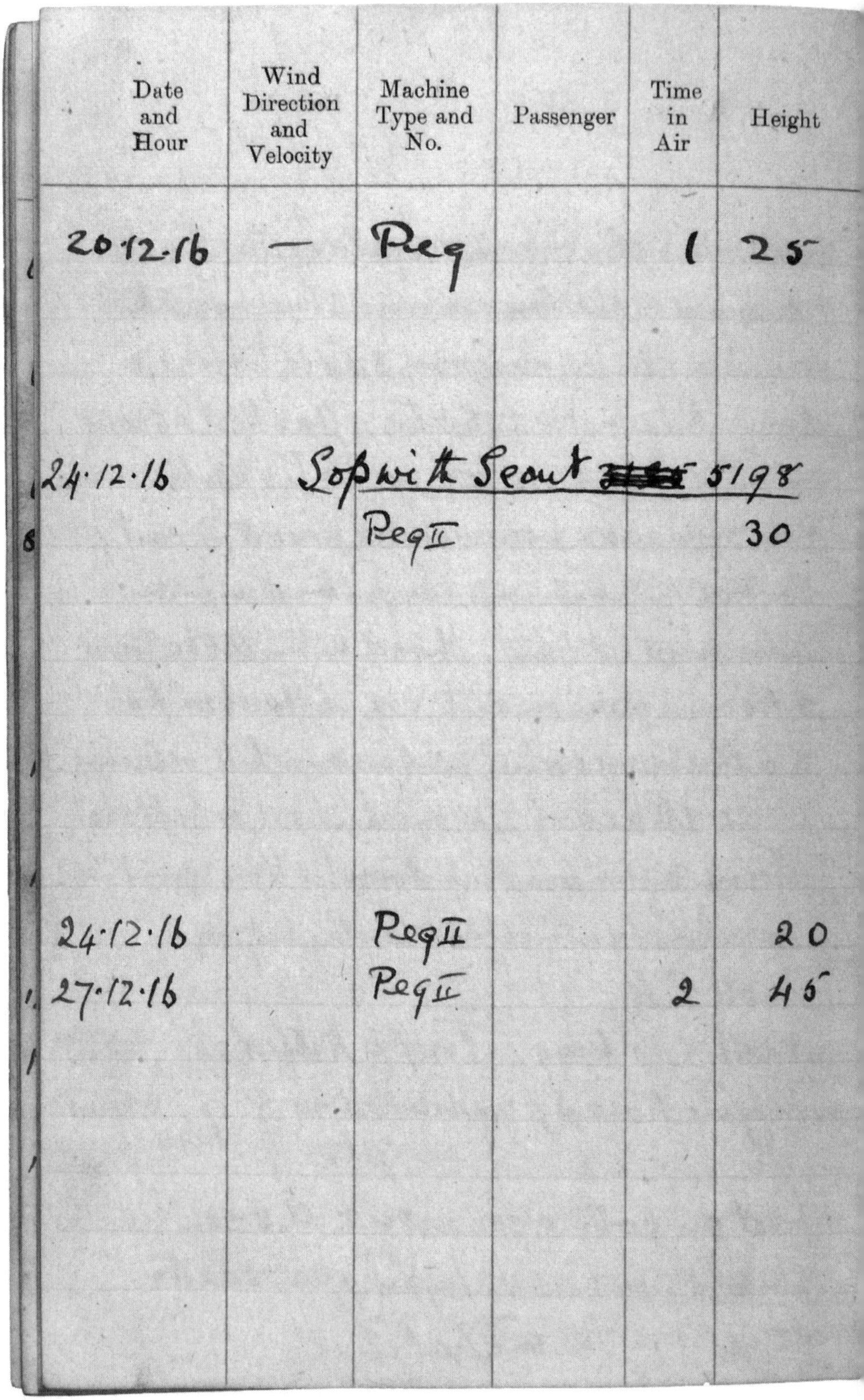

Date and Hour	Wind Direction and Velocity	Machine Type and No.	Passenger	Time in Air	Height
20·12·16	—	Peg		1	25
24·12·16		Sopwith Scout ~~Peg~~ 5198			
		Peg II			30
24·12·16		Peg II			20
27·12·16		Peg II		2	45

Course	Remarks

suddenly the scout above me dived & I got in amongst the 5 Huns below: happened to see a hun on the sights fired & then beat it. outclimbed Type K. them & looked round: saw one machine seesawing down out of control for 2000ft. Suddenly I saw him momentarily regain control but was instantly dived on by a scout & could not see if he regained control permanently, pilot certainly badly wounded if not killed. I don't think I could have got away in Reg I Reg II is certainly a peach for performance dived on another type K on returning but he saw me & I beat it. rejoined formation excellently escorted by Simpson & Cooka 11,000. I remained about 15,000 ft.

attempted O.P. returned

promoted to Flight Commander 1.1.17.

F.St. Todd & Flt.Lt. Croft shot down.

13   MEDICAL RECORDS

This chapter is concerned with those medical records that are not held with records of service. The majority of the following records are from parts of the military medical organizations and the Ministry of Health. Whilst the records described here do not represent everyone who saw service in the flying services, they do represent many ailments and injuries associated with flying and aircraft.

One of the best uses of medical records for the family historian is the placing of an individual in a particular place and on a specific date, and whilst where and how an individual came to be within a medical system may often be less important, the facts can still be of interest or even of great importance.

13.1   Records up to 1918

Records relating to aviation medicine prior to the Second World War are not common. Medical records concerning men of the flying services up to the end of the First World War were primarily created by various service medical organizations, such as those involved in the treatment of battle casualties or in the general medical care of individuals in peace and in war.

13.1.1   ADM 101 Surgeon's Journals

Apart from a few annotations that occur on the records of service of naval officers and RNAS officers in ADM 196 and ADM 273 respectively, and naval ratings records in ADM 188, details relating to individual medical case papers do not exist.

All ship's surgeons had to complete a daily log noting basic details relating to the medical cases they had seen on each day. The majority of records in ADM 101 are for RN warships, but there are a number of logs which either concern ships which are known to have carried aircraft or were kept at Royal Naval Air Service or Fleet Air Arm shore establishments. The following journals are a few examples that can be found in this record series:

Reference	Description	Covering Dates
ADM 101/311	Flying School, Eastchurch	January–August 1914
ADM 101/314	HM Air Station, Isle of Grain, Kent	January–December 1914
ADM 101/316	HM Aviation Service, Expeditionary Force	August–December 1914
ADM 101/332	RN Armoured Car Division	March–December 1915
ADM 101/338	Naval Air Station, Calshot	January–December 1915
ADM 101/371	RN Airship Detachment No.2	July–December 1915
ADM 101/372	RNAS Expeditionary Force, France	January–February 1915
ADM 101/390	No.4 Wing RNAS, France	May–December 1916
ADM 101/390	No.5 Wing RNAS, France	March–December 1916
ADM 101/392	RN Air Station, Redcar	March–December 1916
ADM 101/393	RN Air Station Vendome, France	August–December 1916
ADM 101/394	RN Flying School, Eastchurch	January–March 1916
ADM 101/439	Chingford Air Station	1917
ADM 101/439	Crystal Palace Air Station	1917
ADM 101/441	Dunkirk Air Station	1917
ADM 101/441	Aircraft Depot, France	1917
ADM 101/442	Pulham Air Station	1917
ADM 101/443	Redcar Air Station	1917
ADM 101/443	Tresco Air Station	1917
ADM 101/444	Tipnor Kite Balloon School	1917
ADM 101/444	Vendome Air Station, France	1917
ADM 101/468	Withnoe Air Station	1918

13.1.2 MH 106 Medical Records 1914–18

The Medical Historians' papers in MH 106 consist of a two per cent sample of all of the British Army, and therefore RFC, medical records generated between 1914 and 1919.

The majority of the records concern non-RFC and RAF personnel. However, a number of files deal specifically or partly with sick or wounded of either the RFC or RAF. Most of the records are hospital and casualty clearing station admission books and general casualty records which cover a variety of different parts of the British Army. There are, however, a number of RFC medical sheets relating to both officers and men of the corps who were either wounded or sick in MH 106/2202–6. These records, dated 1916–17, can provide name, rank, number and unit, and a description of the ailment for which the individual was hospitalized:

MH 106/2202	Surnames A–C
MH 106/2203	Surnames D–H
MH 106/2204	Surnames I–O
MH 106/2205	Surnames P–S
MH 106/2206	Surnames T–Z

Admission and other records in MH 106, which include details relating to men and women of the RFC, RNAS, RAF and WRAF, can be found in:

14 FIELD AMBULANCE

MH 106/59	Royal Air Force	May–December 1918

51 FIELD AMBULANCE

MH 106/121	Royal Air Force	August 1918

66 FIELD AMBULANCE

MH 106/153	Royal Air Force	June–September 1918
MH 106/154	Royal Air Force	June–October 1918

139 FIELD AMBULANCE

MH 106/205	Royal Air Force	May–September 1918

3 CASUALTY CLEARING STATION

MH 106/392	Royal Air Force other ranks	June 1918–January 1919
MH 106/393	Royal Air Force other ranks	July 1918–January 1919

11 CASUALTY CLEARING STATION

MH 106/513	Royal Air Force	May 1918–March 1919

31 CASUALTY CLEARING STATION

MH 106/645	Royal Air Force officers	June–December 1918
MH 106/647	Royal Air Force officers and other ranks	March–September 1919
MH 106/652	Royal Air Force other ranks	May–June 1918
MH 106/665	Royal Air Force	August–September 1918

34 CASUALTY CLEARING STATION

MH 106/742	Royal Air Force officers and other ranks	June–December 1918
MH 106/760	Royal Naval Air Service	May–July 1917
MH 106/793	Royal Air Force	June 1918–January 1919
MH 106/794	Royal Air Force officers and other ranks	July 1918–January 1919

39 CASUALTY CLEARING STATION

MH 106/810	Royal Air Force	May–December 1918
MH 106/811	Royal Air Force	January–March 1919

2 General Hospital

MH 106/987	Royal Naval Air Service	February–March 1918
MH 106/1029	Royal Air Force	July–December 1918
MH 106/1030	Royal Air Force officers and other ranks	January–March 1919
MH 106/1034	Royal Air Force other ranks	May–June 1918
MH 106/1035	Royal Air Force officers	July–December 1918
MH 106/1037	Royal Air Force officers and other ranks	January 1919

18 General Hospital

MH 106/1139	Royal Flying Corps	July 1917–January 1918
MH 106/1140	Royal Flying Corps	July–August 1917
MH 106/1141	Royal Flying Corps	August 1917
MH 106/1143	Royal Flying Corps	September–October 1917
MH 106/1145	Royal Flying Corps	October–November 1917
MH 106/1146	Royal Flying Corps	November–December 1917
MH 106/1147	Royal Air Force	December 1917–December 1918
MH 106/1148	Royal Flying Corps and Royal Naval Air Service	February–March 1918
MH 106/1149	Royal Flying Corps	March 1918
MH 106/1153	Royal Flying Corps	April 1918
MH 106/1156	Royal Air Force	April 1918
MH 106/1157	Royal Air Force	April–May 1918
MH 106/1164	Royal Air Force	June 1917–January 1919
MH 106/1180	Royal Air Force other ranks	May 1918–January 1919
MH 106/1187	Royal Air Force	October 1917–March 1918

19 General Hospital

MH 106/1235	Royal Flying Corps	April–May 1916
MH 106/1238–1258	Royal Flying Corps	September 1916–April 1918
MH 106/1259	Royal Air Force	April 1918
MH 106/1260	Royal Air Force	April–May 1918
MH 106/1261	Royal Air Force	May–June 1918
MH 106/1264	Royal Flying Corps	April–June 1916
MH 106/1265	Royal Flying Corps	June–July 1916
MH 106/1266	Royal Flying Corps	July–October 1916
MH 106/1269	Royal Flying Corps	November 1916–March 1917
MH 106/1270	Royal Flying Corps	November 1916–June 1917
MH 106/1281	Royal Air Force	March–December 1918
MH 106/1284	Royal Flying Corps	November 1915–June 1917
MH 106/1288	Royal Flying Corps	June 1916–December 1917
MH 106/1290	Royal Flying Corps	September 1916–August 1917
MH 106/1291	Royal Flying Corps	August–December 1917
MH 106/1292	Royal Flying Corps	January–November 1918

28 General Hospital

MH 106/1316	Royal Flying Corps	August 1916
MH 106/1318	Royal Flying Corps	August 1916
MH 106/1322	Royal Flying Corps	September 1916
MH 106/1333	Royal Flying Corps	March–April 1917
MH 106/1335	Royal Naval Air Service	April–May 1917
MH 106/1337	Royal Flying Corps	May–June 1917
MH 106/1339	Royal Flying Corps	June 1917
MH 106/1340	Royal Flying Corps	June–July 1917
MH 106/1365	Royal Flying Corps	November 1915–October 1916
MH 106/1368	Royal Air Force officers and other ranks	June 1918–April 1919

85 General Hospital

MH 106/1381	Royal Air Force	January–August 1919

4 Stationary Hospital

MH 106/1460	Royal Flying Corps	October–November 1916
MH 106/1483	Royal Air Force	February–April 1918
MH 106/1491	Royal Air Force	1918–19
MH 106/1494	Royal Air Force officers	June 1918–September 1919
MH 106/1497	Women's Royal Air Force	April–September 1919

County of Middlesex War Hospital at Napsbury

MH 106/1528	Royal Air Force	March 1918–June 1919
MH 106/1529	Royal Air Force	November 1918–July 1919
MH 106/1530	Royal Air Force	May 1918–April 1919

Queen Alexandra's Military Hospital Millbank

MH 106/1636	Royal Air Force	April–December 1918
MH 106/1637	Royal Air Force officers	April–December 1918
MH 106/1638	Royal Air Force cadets and other ranks	January–April 1919
MH 106/1639	Royal Air Force officers	January–May 1919
MH 106/1690	Royal Air Force	June–August 1917
MH 106/1691	Royal Air Force	August–October 1917
MH 106/1692	Royal Air Force	October–December 1917

Catterick Military Hospital

MH 106/1825	Royal Air Force officers and other ranks	June 1918–December 1919
MH 106/1899	Royal Air Force officers	January 1918–February 1919

CRAIGLOCKHART HOSPITAL

MH 106/1900	Royal Air Force	July 1918–January 1919
MH 106/1901	Royal Air Force	August 1918
MH 106/2037	Royal Air Force other ranks	June–July 1918

31 AMBULANCE TRAIN

MH 106/2038	Royal Air Force officers	June–July 1918
MH 106/2040	Royal Air Force other ranks	July 1918–April 1919

13.2 Inter-war Records

Records containing medical information for the period between the two world wars are really confined to the Admiralty Surgeon's Journals in ADM 101. From the period c.1914 the journals are arranged and described by ranges of name, either ship, place or unit, and in chronological order, year on year. It may be necessary to look for an ADM 101 piece description likely to contain the item you seek, rather than just keyword searching the ADM 101 catalogue.

Many of the Admiralty Surgeon's Journals are for HM ships that carried single aircraft launched from a catapult, as well as aircraft carriers and Royal Naval Air Stations. Many of the Royal Naval Air Stations are listed by their placename (locations), but some are listed by their HMS name. A list of Royal Naval Air Stations and their associated HM names can be found in Appendix 4.

13.3 Second World War Records

Medical records of the Second World War can be found in many of the series already mentioned, most notably ADM 101, but there are a few others.

The war diaries of Army medical units can be found in the series WO 177 and WO 222. Whilst not mentioning Army flying units specifically, you may find details of men of the AAC, GPR and SAS amongst the diaries.

More detailed reports of Army medical units rather than the day-to-day accounts of the war diaries, may be found in WO 222. Once again, these reports do not mention specific Army flying units and organizations by name.

The Operational Record Books of RAF medical units can be found in the series AIR 29. It is possible to search for these units by placename or designation on the Catalogue.

13.3.1 *AIR 49 RAF Medical Services*

This record series contains records created by the Air Ministry, covering all aspects of medicine in the Royal Air Force. Most of the records are concerned with general medical policy and medical studies, rather than individuals, but it is possible to find people mentioned in a number of files. For example, the history of RAF Hospital Wroughton in AIR 49/322 contains the names of key staff in an appendix at the end of the file. Medical histories of various RAF units can be found in this series, but they are concerned with the medical state of a unit and the types of cases that occurred in that unit only.

13.4   Post-Second World War Medical Records

Further Admiralty Surgeon's Journals can be found in ADM 101, but the majority for 1946 onwards are currently closed.

Operational Record Books for RAF medical units can now be found in AIR 29.

Details of operational matters concerning medical units post-1945 can be found in chapter 8.

14 PHOTOGRAPHS

As a photograph archive, the National Archives holds some very rare and unusual photographs connected with aviation. Although there are images of numerous individuals, these are usually in unnamed groups rather than named portrait type photographs.

The variety of images the National Archives holds is reflected in the 'In Camera' books that were published by Sutton Publishing. Although not all of the photographs have come from the National Archives, these guides do show what is likely to be found. Another rich source is the PRO's *RAF in Action 1939–1945: Images from Air Cameras and War Artists* by Roy Conyers Nesbit.

There are numerous different record series where photographs may be found. Those that have been discovered have been listed in a photograph catalogue that can be found in the Open Reading Room.

Fig. 43 *A typical example of a non-operational type photograph found amongst the records books of miscellaneous units in* AIR 29. AIR 29/575

A number of photographs have been extracted from their original homes and placed into new collections. Photographs extracted from AIR record series have been put into the record series CN 5, and those extracted from the AVIA record series have been put into CN 6.

It is possible to find photographs of famous individuals. Beyond looking in the photograph catalogue, you can use an individual's surname as part of a keyword search on the Catalogue.

Many operational records contain photographs of the results of aircraft action. The ORBs of training units in AIR 29 contain many course photographs of trainee aircrew. Many of the photographs in AIR 29 are not captioned, so locating a photograph of a specific named individual is almost impossible.

The Fleet Air Arm squadron operational records in ADM 207 are another rich source of photographs. Not only do these records contain group photographs of personnel, they also contain of images of aircraft, flying, static or even some that had crashed.

Admiralty Surgeon's Journals in ADM 101 can contain images of particular interest relating to injuries sustained by personnel whilst involved with aircraft.

Fig. 44 *The personnel of 804 Squadron Fleet Air Arm.* ADM 207/8

For more advice about the photographic holdings of the National Archives you may wish to contact staff in the Image Library.

15 RECORDS HELD BY OTHER INSTITUTIONS

15.1 Fleet Air Arm Museum

The Fleet Air Arm Museum at Yeovilton houses the greatest collection of aircraft, archives and artefacts connected with British naval aviation anywhere in the world. Many of the aircraft on display are unique to Europe, and many are the sole example of their type in the world.

For those interested in research into aircraft and personnel of the RNAS and FAA, the museum has an unrivalled collection, which continues to grow. Indeed the archival staff assisted me with my own research, for which I am most grateful. The museum can be contacted at:

Fleet Air Arm Museum
RNAS Yeovilton
Ilchester
Somerset BA22 8HT
Tel: 01935 840565
www.fleetairarm.com

15.2 Royal Engineers Museum

The corps museum of the Royal Engineers houses numerous displays about all aspects of the life and history of the corps. Included in the displays, as one might imagine, are those concerning aviation, not only from the balloon era but also into the late 20th century. Also included in the displays is an unrivalled collection of medals awarded to members of the corps. The RE Museum is at:

Brompton Barracks
Prince Arthur Road
Gillingham
Kent ME4 4UG
Tel: 01634 822839,
www.remuseum.org.uk

15.3 Museum of Army Flying

Found at the home of the Army Air Corps, at Middle Wallop in Hampshire, this museum is primarily concerned with Army aviation in the 20th century. Displays concerning both the Glider Pilot Regiment and Air Observation Posts, together with those concerning the post-1957 Army Air Corps, are to be found in the museum, along with examples of related aircraft and gliders. The museum has a library and archive where it is possible to research various aspects of Army aviation. Enquiries concerning the archives should be made to the curator (tel: 01980 674339, *archives@flying-museum.org.uk*). The address of the museum is:

Fig. 45 *Allied women pilots—three American and one Polish—of the Air Transport Auxiliary Service in the Second World War leave an airfield near Maidenhead.*

Museum of Army Flying
Middle Wallop
Stockbridge
Hampshire
SO20 8DY
Tel: 01264 784421
www.flying-museum.org.uk

15.4 Airborne Forces Museum

The Airborne Forces Museum at Aldershot in Hampshire housed various displays concerning the activities of troops of the British Army who arrived at their area of operations by air. Consequently the displays contained numerous items concerning the Glider Pilot Regiment.

The Airborne Forces Museum has now closed and will reopen in a new museum provisionally called Airborne Assault–Duxford at the Imperial War Museum site at Duxford in late 2008.

Contact the Imperial War Museum for further information.

15.5 Imperial War Museum

The Imperial War Museum (IWM), which was founded in 1917, not only displays a wide variety of items concerning warfare in the 20th century but also holds extensive archives. Split into a number of different departments, the IWM holds a vast array of archival material that may be of use to a researcher. Departments of Documents, Printed Books, Photographs and Sound may all provide the researcher with further information. The IWM is also responsible for the former RAF airfield at Duxford in Cambridgeshire. It is possible to search the catalogue of IWM holdings via their website. To obtain further details about access to the IWM contact:

Imperial War Museum
Lambeth Road
London SE1 6HZ
Tel: 020 7416 5000
www.iwm.org.uk

15.6 Royal Air Force Museum

The Royal Air Force Museum was opened in 1972 and contains displays from the earliest days of Army aviation in the 19th century to the present. The library and archive of the museum holds a wide range of material relating to personnel of the RFC and RAF. By far the most important collection relating to pilots is the collection of photographs of holders of Royal Aero Club certificates.

The RAF Museum is the recognized place of deposit of a number of public records. Amongst these are the records of the RAF Staff College at Andover. These can be found listed at the National Archives in the series AIR 69.

Perhaps one of the most significant collections held by Hendon relating to the Second World War is the records of service of the Air Transport Auxiliary. These records are subject to data protection and as such are only open to subject individuals and next of kin.

Beyond the photographs, there are collections of casualty records for the First and Second World Wars, and a collection of Air Ministry Bulletins which contain basic biographical data relating to members of the RAF who received awards between 1939 and 1959.

For information about access to the archives contact the Department of Research and Information Services. The RAF Museum is located at:

Royal Air Force Museum
Graham Park Way
Hendon
London
NW9 5LL
Tel: 020 8205 2266
www.rafmuseum.org.uk

15.7   Commonwealth War Graves Commission

The Commonwealth (formerly Imperial) War Graves Commission is responsible for the care and maintenance of cemeteries and memorials concerning the dead, primarily of the two world wars. The Commission holds most of its records on computer and the information they contain can be obtained either by writing to the Commission or by accessing its website. The Commission is at:

The Commonwealth War Graves Commission
2 Marlow Road
Maidenhead
Berkshire
SL6 7DX
Tel: 01628 634221
www.cwgc.org

APPENDIX.

PERSONNEL.

	August 1914.			December 1916.			December 1917.			October 1918.		
	Officers.	Other Ranks.	Total.	Officers.	Other Ranks.	Total.	Officers.	Other Ranks.	Total.	Officers.	Other Ranks.	Total.
R.F.C. ..	147	1,097	1,244	5,982	51,915	57,897	15,522	98,738	114,260	..	..	..
R.N.A.S. ..	50	550	600	2,764	26,129	28,893	4,765	43,050	47,815	..	..	..
Royal Air Force	..	..	..	..	..	..	..	..	..	27,906	263,842	291,748
Total ..	..	..	1,844	..	..	86,790	..	..	162,075	..	..	291,748

MACHINES AND ENGINES ON CHARGE.

	August 1914.		January 1917.		January 1918.		October 1918.	
	Machines.	Engines.	Machines.	Engines.	Machines.	Engines.	Machines.	Engines.
R.F.C. ..	179	..	3,929	6,056	8,350	14,755	..	..
R.N.A.S. ..	93	..	1,567	3,672	2,741	6,902	..	..
R.A.F. ..	..	..	..	..	..	..	22,171	37,702
Total ..	272	..	5,496	9,728	11,091	21,657	22,171	37,702

OUTPUT OF MACHINES AND ENGINES.

	August 1914 to May 1915 (10 months).		June 1915 to February 1917 (21 months).		March 1917 to December 1917 (10 months).		January 1918 to October 1918 (10 months).	
	Machines.	Engines.	Machines.	Engines.	Machines.	Engines.	Machines.	Engines.
R.F.C. ..	530	141	7,137	8,917	12,275	..	..	..
R.N.A.S. ..	No record.	No record	No record	No record	1,246	..	..	..
R.A.F. ..	..	..	..	..	..	..	26,685	29,561
Total ..	530	141	7,137	8,917	13,521	13,979	26,685	29,561

Fig. 46 *An illustration by personnel numbers of how the RFC/RAF expanded between 1914 and 1918.*
AIR 1/686/21/13/2252

16 RESEARCH TECHNIQUES

There are many ways to begin researching the career and experiences of those involved with military aviation. Perhaps the most important and yet most obvious starting point is to know when the individual served, as this will dictate where you begin your research.

The three armed services each create records relating to military aviation in their own way and this will dictate how you approach them. For instance, the Royal Navy (RNAS) records start at the date when a person joined; the Army (RE Balloon section) order records by when a person left; and the RAF organize records for RAF officers and airwomen alphabetically, while those for RAF airmen are ordered by number.

There are always variations, but when you are working with the records of thousands of men and women, this is bound to happen.

16.1 Printed Sources

There are numerous printed sources containing information about all aspects of military aviation, from information about particular aircraft types to unit histories, books about particular events in aviation history, such as the Battle of Britain or the Dambuster raid, and almost anything aircraft-related you can think of. It is not the intention here to highlight all of those books that may be of interest to the aviation or family historian, rather to discuss the key official printed sources and those works readily available or in the Library of the National Archives.

The first place to look are the *Lists*. All officers and warrant officers (depending upon date) of the Army, Navy and Royal Air Force are listed in their respective *List*. All of these *List*s are arranged in their own particular way and depending upon the date the information within them may be very brief or, if you are lucky, a little more detailed. The majority of these *List*s are available on the open shelves in the Open Reading Room. However, some editions of the *Navy List* are in the entrance to the Document Reading Room.

Fig. 47 (facing and overleaf) *Report on operations in Afghanistan 1928–9.* AIR 5/857

EAST INDIA (MILITARY).

Report on the
Air Operations in Afghanistan
between December 12th, 1928, and
February 25th, 1929.

Presented by the Secretary of State for India
to Parliament by Command of His Majesty.

September, 1929.

LONDON:
PRINTED AND PUBLISHED BY HIS MAJESTY'S STATIONERY OFFICE.
To be purchased directly from H.M. STATIONERY OFFICE at the following addresses:
Adastral House, Kingsway, London, W.C.2; 120, George Street, Edinburgh;
York Street, Manchester; 1, St. Andrew's Crescent, Cardiff;
15, Donegall Square West, Belfast;
or through any Bookseller.

1929.

Price 9d. net.

Cmd. 3400.

APPENDIX "D."

ROYAL AIR FORCE.

Record of Aeroplanes and Pilots concerned in the evacuation from Kabul between 23rd December, 1928, and 25th February, 1929, and the loads evacuated.

Date.	Type.	Pilot.	Passengers Evacuated.	Baggage Evacuated.	Total Load.
				lbs.	lbs.
December 23rd...	Victoria	S./Lr. Maxwell	21	200	1,800
Do. ...	Wapiti	S./Lr. Nicholas (W./T.)..	—	—	—
Do. ...	D. H. 9 A	F./Lt. Prendergast ...	—	120	120
Do. ...	Do.	F./Lt. Pelly	—	120	120
Do. ...	Do.	F./O. Fuller-Good ...	—	150	150
December 24th...	Wapiti	F./O. Russell - Stracey (W./T.)	—		
Do. ...	D. H. 9 A	S./Lr. Bailey	1	70	210
Do. ...	Do.	F./Lt. Prendergast ...	1	100	250
Do. ...	Do.	F./O. Fuller-Good ...	1	100	230
Do. ...	Do.	F./O. Butcher	1	80	220
Do. ...	Do.	F./O. McKee	1	75	225
Do. ...	Do.	Sgt. Davis	1	100	230
Do. ...	Do.	S./Ldr. Neville	1	100	260
Do. ...	Do.	F./O. Wisher	1	100	230
Do. ...	Do.	F./O. Jenkens	1	111	250
Do. ...	Do.	P./O. Horner	1	90	210
Do. ...	Do.	F./Sgt. Steers	1	100	250
Do. ...	Victoria	S.L. Maxwell	10	250	1,600
December 26th...	D. H. 9 A	W./Cr. Murlis-Green ...	1	100	250
Do. ...	Do.	F./O. Spreckley	1	90	240
Do. ...	Do.	F./O. Jenkins	1	80	210
Do. ...	Do.	Sgt. Howells (W./T.) ...	—	—	—
Do. ...	Victoria	S./Lr. Maxwell	23	460	1,680
December 29th...	Hinaidi	F./Lt. Anderson ...	11	500	1,605
Do. ...	Victoria	S./Lr. Maxwell	26	30	1,600
December 30th...	Do.	S./Lr. Maxwell	11	200	1,550
Do. ...	Do.	F./O. Anness	11	100	1,565
January 1st ...	Do.	F./O. Anness	7	300	1,400
January 9th ...	Do.	S./Lr. Maxwell	5	400	1,300
January 18th ...	Do.	S./Lr. Maxwell	7	80	1,000
Do. ...	Do.	F./Lt. Chapman ...	5	125	950
January 19th ...	Do.	S./Lr. Maxwell	7	300	1,200
Do. ...	Do.	F./O. Anness	6	200	1,280
January 29th ...	Hinaidi	F./Lt. Anderson (Remained at Kabul).	—	—	—
Do. ...	Victoria	F./Lt. Chapman. (Forced landed near Sarobi).	—	—	—
January 31st ...	Do.	F./O. Anness	8	180	1,380
February 1st ...	Do.	F./O. Anness	10	200	1,600
Do. ...	Do.	S./Lr. Maxwell	11	220	1,600
February 3rd ...	Do.	F./O. Anness	12	180	1i475
Do. ...	Do.	S./Lr. Maxwell	10	697	1,800
Do. ...	Hinaidi	F./Lt. Anderson ...	1	700	900
February 4th ...	Victoria	S./Lr. Maxwell	9	580	1,595
Do. ...	Do.	F./O. Anness	18	200	1,630

The *Confidential Air Force List* and *Air Ministry Air Force List* are in the series AIR 10 and have to be ordered on the document-ordering computers.

16.1.1 The Army List

For officers serving in the RE Balloon Section and Royal Flying Corps up to early 1918, the *Army List* is the first *List* to consult. Each *List* includes a name index. In many cases during the First World War you may find an officer listed under his original regiment/corps as well as under the Royal Flying Corps. Apart from confirming the fact that an individual was in a particular regiment/corps, any *Army List* entry will provide you with the date of commission at a particular rank. The date of commission is very important for officers of the Royal Engineers who were commissioned prior to 1915, as their records of service in WO 25/3913–20 are arranged by commission date.

16.1.2 The Navy List

Royal Naval Air Service and Fleet Air Arm officers are listed in the *Navy List*. Once again the *List* is name-indexed, but unlike the *Army List* that has one index, the *Navy List* has separate name indexes for Royal Navy (including RNAS) and Royal Marine officers, another index for officers of the Royal Naval Reserve and another for officers of the Royal Naval Volunteer Reserve. Apart from listing the officers on various ships during the First World War, a list of officers in RNAS squadrons may also be found.

The only way of identifying officers of the Fleet Air Arm during the Second World War is to look at their specialization, which should be (A).

When using post-Second World War *Navy Lists*, officers with the specialisation of 'P' for Pilot or 'O' for Observer can help to identify officers of the Fleet Air Arm.

16.1.3 The Air Force List and the Confidential Air Force List

The earliest *Air Force List* was published in 1918 when the service was first created. The arrangement of the *Air Force List* has varied over its existence, but there is always a name index that will give you a column or page number where basic information about the officer may be found.

Between the two world wars the *Air Force List* details the officers in individual squadrons and in other units, such as Armoured Car Units. Once the Second World War started this sort of information ceased being published.

The *Air Force List* of the Second World War period became a substantial publication but did little more than list the officers in the service. Details of officers serving in non-flying duties and, in many cases, the more senior parts of the RAF hierarchy can be found in the *Confidential Air Force List*. These lists cover the period April 1939–1954 and can be found in AIR 10/3814–40, 5237–56, 5413–21 and 5581–2. Similar lists for 1955–6 can be found in AIR 10/7360–72.

All of these lists have named indexes and can provide you with information that may lead you to the RAF Station Record Books in AIR 28 and Miscellaneous Record Books in AIR 29.

Perhaps one of the most useful aspects of the *Air Force List* from 1941 onwards is the appearance of an RAF officer's service number. This number can be used to search the *London Gazette* (see below).

A graduation list of Polish officers for 1943 can be found in AIR 10/3843.

Post-Second World War *Air Force List*s did not return to the pre-war level of information, showing who served with which unit or organization. However, the post-1945 editions of the *Air Force List* do incorporate a '*Retired List*' that provides date of birth, date of commission, highest rank attained and date of retirement. Eventually a separate '*Retired List*' was created and this is still published. By following an officer through the *RAF Retired List* it is, in most cases, possible to discover the date of death of an officer.

16.1.4 *The Royal Canadian Air Force List*

Seven editions of the *Royal Canadian Air Force List* can be found on the shelves of the Library at the National Archives. These editions, similar to the Second World War *Air Force List*, cover the years 1940, 1942, 1943, 1944, 1945, 1946 and 1960.

16.1.5 *Casualties: the end as the beginning*

It is a sad fact that, in many cases, it can be easier to research someone who died in service after a short career, rather than a man who served over 20 years without a black mark against his name.

Apart from *Airmen Died in the Great War* mentioned above, perhaps one of the most useful published works concerning allied airmen who became air casualties in the First World War is *The Sky Their Battlefield* by T. Henshaw. Name-indexed, the book not only lists those who died; it also lists those who were captured.

During the Second World War alone, over 55,000 airmen of Bomber Command died on active service. If you do not know the squadron an individual was serving in at the time of death, your research may be very frustrating.

A number of books have been compiled by such authors as Bill Chorley and Norman Franks and published by Midland Publishing covering the losses of the various RAF commands during the Second World War.

Arranged by date, it is possible to find out who died on any given date, the type of aircraft they were in, the squadron the aircraft came from and the names of others (as appropriate) who died in the same aircraft. These books quite often record other facts not normally found in the operational records books in AIR 27 and AIR 29, such as whether a member or members of a crew did survive and fall into enemy hands.

The three key series of 'Losses' books are as follows and they are regularly updated.

Bomber Command Losses
Fighter Command Losses
Coastal Command Losses

The *Bomber Command Losses* series also includes separate volumes for the training units as well as those for operational squadrons.

16.1.6 *The start of the air service*
Being connected with a new service upon its formation must have been quite a thing and items such as medals connected with these pioneering individuals are much sought after.

Information about the first 1200 or so RFC airmen who joined the Royal Flying Corps prior to the outbreak of the First World War can be found in *Contemptible Little Flying Corps* by I. McInnes and J. Webb.

16.1.7 *Aces*
A pilot or gunner who destroyed five or more enemy aircraft was considered an 'ace'. There are two published works covering British aces of the two world wars.

Above The Trenches: A Complete Record of the Fighter Aces and Units of the British Empire Forces, 1915–1920 by C. Shores, N. Franks and R. Guest lists in alphabetical order the success of the aces of the First World War period, with each entry giving details that can be used to consult the operational records in AIR 1.

Aces High by C. Shores and C. Williams provides information about allied aces in the Second World War and provides information that can be used to access records in AIR 27 and AIR 50, for example.

16.1.8 *The Distinguished Flying Cross*
The most common award for gallantry in the Second World War was the Distinguished Flying Cross (DFC). A roll of the DFC, *The Distinguished Flying Cross and How it Was Won 1918–1995* by N. and C. Carter, is a useful source as it publishes the immediate award citations and provides unit details.

The Distinguished Flying Medal Register for the Second World War by I. Tavender is very useful inasmuch as it provides TNA document references where the recommendations can be found.

16.1.9 *Images of aviators*

Deciphering images of military men in uniform requires knowledge and skills that have been acquired over time. After the First World War it becomes much easier to identify an RAF officer or airman, but because of the complex nature of the flying services and their uniforms between 1914 and 1918 a useful reference source is needed. By unlocking the photograph of a First World War period aviator you will be able to research in the most effective place first. Consulting *British Air Forces 1914–1918* by A. and P. Cormack should help you to work out if a First World War period aviator is RFC, RNAS or RAF.

16.2 The *London Gazette* Online

The *London Gazette* is the official newspaper of the state and has been so since 1665. Various announcements relating to state matters are announced in the paper, including military commissions, promotions and honours and awards. The term 'gazetted' in the context of commissions and honours and awards means the date upon which the event was announced in the *London Gazette*.

There are a number of ways to access the *London Gazette* at the National Archives. The series ZJ 1 contains the paper from 1665 onwards. Depending upon the date, a single piece of ZJ 1 may cover a whole year, although during the two world wars it covers only a single month.

The most popular editions of the *London Gazette* are those for the two world wars. These are available on microfilm on open access in the Open Reading Room.

It is now possible to search the complete *London Gazette* online via *www.gazettes-online.co.uk*. The papers can be searched by keyword, which may be the name of an individual, a service number or even a term that is likely to appear in the body of the text.

In the context of the Second World War it is possible to search the *London Gazette* by an RAF service number. This is a very effective way of locating items of interest, especially when the full name of the individual is either unknown or the paper only uses initial(s) and surname.

16.3   Aids to Research

The following lists and charts are for handy reference and can be used as a starting point for research. The series listed under each heading are key places to direct research, but are not comprehensive.

16.3.1   *Records of service*

RE BALLOON SECTION

Officers (*Army List* first)	Other Ranks (discharged 1883–1900/1900–13)
WO 25	WO 97

RFC

Officers (*Army List* first)	Other Ranks
WO 25/WO 76	WO 97 (discharged 1912/1913)
WO 339/WO 374	WO 363/WO 364 (discharged 1914–31/3/1918)
AIR 76 (alphabetical order on microfilm)	AIR 79 (numbers up to 329000)

RNAS

Officers (name search ADM 273 on Catalogue) (*Navy List* for early officers for ADM 196)	Ratings (up to 31/3/1918)
ADM 273/ADM 196	ADM 188 (on DocumentsOnline)

RAF

Officers	Airmen	Airwomen
AIR 76 (alphabetical order on microfilm)	AIR 79 (numbers up to 329000)	AIR 80 (alphabetical order on DocumentsOnline)

16.3.2   *Operational records*

RE BALLOON SECTION
WO 32, WO 33, WO 105 and WO 108

RFC
AIR 1 and WO 158

RNAS
ADM 1, ADM 116, ADM 137 and AIR 1

RAF

First World War	Inter-war Years	Second World War	Post-Second World War
AIR 1, AIR 5, AIR 20 and AIR 27	AIR 5, AIR 8, AIR 10, AIR 20, AIR 23 and AIR 27	AIR 20, AIR 14, AIR 15, AIR 16, AIR 23, AIR 27, AIR 37 and AIR 50	AIR 10, AIR 20 and AIR 27 (up to 1980)

16.3.3 Orders, decorations and medals

	Campaign Medals	Order and Decorations	Long Service Medals
RE Balloon Section	WO 100	WO 105, WO 108	WO 102
RFC	WO 329	AIR 1	WO 102
RNAS	ADM 171	ADM 1, ADM 116, ADM 137, AIR 1	ADM 171
RAF	—	AIR 1, AIR 2	AIR 72
FAA	—	ADM 1, ADM 116, ADM 199	ADM 171
AAC	—	WO 373	—

16.3.4 Training of aircrew

During the Second World War, RAF aircrew usually went through a process that took them through various units. If you know the specific unit, it is possible to find an Operational Records Book for that unit in the appropriate records series (most probably AIR 29 or AIR 27). The various stages in the training process were as follows:

Aircrew Selection Board
Initial Training Wing
Elementary Training
Advanced Training
Operational Training/Conversion Training
Squadron

ORBs for the first five stages can be found in AIR 29 and squadron ORBs can be found in AIR 27.

Due to the restricted air space over Britain and the threat of attack from German aircraft, much aircrew training was undertaken overseas, especially in Canada and parts of Africa.

16.3.5 Operational Record Books

If you find an individual in an Operational Record Book (ORB), there is a technique you can use to follow their career but it only works if the information is recorded.

By knowing when an individual served in a particular unit or squadron, by using the ORBs in AIR 27 or AIR 29, it is possible to follow their presence in that unit over a period of time by looking for their names in the crew of an aircraft. In either the monthly summary of the appendices, individuals posted into or out of a unit are usually listed, either saying where they have come from or where they are going to. By looking at the ORB for the place an individual came from or was posted to, it may then be possible to follow them over long periods of time.

Unfortunately, the technique described above is best suited to aircrew rather than those who spent their careers on the ground. However, personnel serving in any unit where an ORB exists may also be pursued.

16.3.6 *Operational codenames*

Many military operations since the mid-20th century have been planned, executed and assessed under the cloak of a codename. Many of these codenames have slipped through unnoticed by the public, but others have become well known.

When searching the Catalogue for records by using a codename, rather than restricting the search to AIR, you can start the search by leaving the department box of the search page blank. Many operations in the Second World War involved more than one service and consequently records may be spread across ADM, AIR, CAB, DEFE AND WO.

Of all the codenames used in the 20th century in relation to military aviation, the following are worth noting.

Chastise	Dambuster raid, May 1943
Crossbow	Attacks on V Weapons launching sites, 1944
Freshman	Attack on the heavy water plant in Norway, 1942
Gomorrah	Fire raid on Hamburg, 1943
Husky	Invasion of Sicily, 1943
Manna	Food drops on Holland, 1945
Millennium	1000-bomber raid on Cologne, 1943
Market Garden	Attack on Arnhem, 1944
Overlord	D-Day landings, 1944
Varsity	Rhine crossing, 1945

A search of the Catalogue for Freshman, for example, produces five results in AIR records but another 14 spread across CAB, DEFE, HS and WO, so a wide search may be the best way to start.

16.3.7 *Further avenues*

In the electronic age, searching for published books and articles and websites devoted to military aviation and the RFC, RNAS and RAF and its operations in particular has never been easier and more rewarding. Such is the enthusiasm for the RAF in particular that the number of websites is always growing. However, as researchers, which site do you trust, since the information in them has to be sourced from somewhere?

The current Ministry of Defence website, *www.mod.uk*, is a very good place to start researching RAF operations and, to a lesser degree, personnel. There are links to various RAF pages about RAF history and current operations and the same can be said for the Fleet Air Arm and Army Air Corps.

In order to find websites that may be of use in your research, just use your favourite search engine. You will be surprised how often you will end up at the National Archives website!

Published unit histories are a very good source of information, especially if the person you are researching was part of an aircrew. A useful way of finding out if there is a published unit history, beyond using a library catalogue or a bookseller's website, is to see if there is a squadron association and then contact them. Many RAF squadron associations have a unit historian.

There are a number of associations concerned with aviation history and the following two are worthy of note.

Air Britain (*www.air-britain.com*) was formed in 1948 and its members are interested in various aspect of aviation, but aircraft is one of the core areas. The society has published numerous works on British military aircraft and aviation; many of the books contain information about those who flew and operated them. A number of books written by Ray Sturtivant and published by Air Britain are available in the Library at the National Archives.

Cross and Cockade International (*www.crossandcockade.com*) is a First World War aviation society and its journal is available in the Library at the National Archives. Articles in the society's journal cover both unit and individual histories.

Records covering various aspects of the RAF's operations in India and information about the Royal Indian Air Force are held in the India Office collection at the British Library. Access to the British Library reading rooms is by ticket. For more information see *www.bl.uk* or write to:

The British Library
96 Euston Road
London
NW1 2DB

Order of Merit	Squadron No.	Date of formation	Late function	Remarks
1	206	January 1917 as No. 6 (Naval) Squadron	Single Seater Fighter. Day bomber.	Formed at Dunkirk as No. 6 Squadron, R.N.A.S., for service with the R.F.C. on the Western Front. Was disbanded as a fighter squadron owing to shortage of pilots in August 1917, but was re-formed as a day bomber, equipped with D.H.9 (B.H.P.) aeroplanes in November 1917. Recrossed to France in January 1918. Thence until the Armistice the squadron was engaged on distant photography and bombing. On one day during this period 5½ tons of bombs were dropped on enemy targets. The squadron, during 1918, had a very fine record.
2	228 (229,273)x	Yarmouth air station. Original formation April 1913.	Marine operational unit. Anti-submarine and anti-zeppelin patrols over North Sea area. Flying boats and float seaplanes.	Yarmouth was one of the six original stations to be established by the Naval Wing of the R.F.C. and had a high tradition. The flying boats, seaplanes and aeroplanes of the unit did consistently good work during the war against Zeppelins, (of which three were destroyed) submarines and German aircraft over the North Sea.
3	240	Calshot seaplane station. Original formation March 1913.	Marine operational unit. Anti-submarine patrols of Channel and convoy escort by flying boats and float seaplanes.	Calshot was the third of the original stations to be established by the Naval Wing of the R.F.C. Was the centre of early seaplane experimental work, bomb dropping and firing from the air.
4	220 (221,222,223)x	Squadrons of the original No. 2 Wing, R.N.A.S. which was formed in June 1915.	Air operations in the Aegean. Fighting and day bombing.	These squadrons, known originally as 'A', 'B', 'C' and 'D' Squadrons, formed No. 2 Wing of the R.N.A.S. for service in the Dardanelles and Asia Minor, and against the Bulgarian and Turkish lines of communication in Macedonia and Turkey from August 1915 onwards.
5	269	Parent unit R.N.A.S. base at Port Said formed in January 1916.	Day bomber.	R.N.A.S. command at Port Said did very valuable reconnaissance work and bombing attacks during the campaign in Sinai and Palestine against the Turkish lines of communication, and also in spotting for H.M. Ships bombarding the enemy positions.
6	102	August 1917.	Short night bomber.	Crossed to France in September 1917. Very valuable night bombing and reconnaissance of enemy communications during 1918. Between 21st March and the end of October 1918 the squadron dropped 317 tons of bombs in 218 raids, or an average of 2¼ tons of bombs per night.
7	59	1st August 1916.	Corps Reconnaissance Squadron.	Squadron went to France on 13th February 1917. Had a consistently good record in France, and on one occasion received a telegram of congratulations from Sir Douglas Haig. Did particularly good tactical reconnaissance work during the first day of the German offensive of March 1918. During the final Allied advance one pilot of the squadron attacked an enemy gun, killing the gunners and horses, and capturing the gun (77 m.m.) as a trophy.
8	53	May 1916.	Corps Reconnaissance.	Flew to France on the 26th December 1916. Attached to IX Corps. Played a prominent part in the Battle of Messines, and received the congratulations of the Second Army Corps. Low bombing and reconnaissance duty during the German offensives of 1918, and worked in co-operation with the X Corps in the final Allied advance in the summer and autumn of 1918.
9	63	31st August 1916.	Corps Reconnaissance.	Went to Mesopotamia in July 1917. Did very valuable work during the last year of the campaign in that country and also in Persia under trying conditions.
10	98	30th August 1917.	Day bomber.	Crossed to France at the end of March 1918 in time to take an active part in the Battles of the Lys. On the 12th April 3¼ tons of bombs were dropped during seven raids. The squadron had a good fighting and bombing record in 1918, and, in all, between April and November 84½ tons of bombs were expended by the unit.
11	217	January 1918.	Day bomber. Anti-submarine patrols.	When the use of seaplanes for patrols of the Flanders Bight became too hazardous, the seaplane base at Dunkirk was disbanded and No. 17 Squadron, R.N.A.S., (later 217 R.A.F.) equipped with D.H.4 aeroplanes, was formed to continue this duty. Many submarines were sighted and attacked during 1918, as were also German T.B.D.'s off Zeebrugge and Ostend. Valuable work during naval blocking operations at Zeebrugge and Ostend in April and May 1918.

Fig. 48 *Particulars of wartime service of RAF squadrons operating on 11 Nov 1918.*
AIR 1/686/21/13/2251

APPENDIX 1

Ranks in the Royal Air Force

<small>COMMISSIONED RANKS</small>

RNAS 1912–18	RFC 1912–18 and RAF 1918–19	RAF 1919–present day	WAAF and WRAF 1939–67[1]
		Marshal of the Royal Air Force[2]	
General		Air Chief Marshal	
Lieutenant General		Air Marshal	
Major General		Air Vice-Marshal	Air Chief Commandant
Brigadier		Air Commodore	Air Commandant
Wing Captain	Colonel	Group Captain	Group Officer
Wing Commander	Lieutenant Colonel	Wing Commander	Wing Officer
Major		Squadron Leader	Squadron Officer
Flight Lieutenant	Captain	Flight Lieutenant	Flight Officer
Flight Sub-Lieutenant	Lieutenant	Flying Officer	Section Officer[3]
Second Lieutenant		Pilot Officer	Assistant Section Officer[4]

Princess Mary's Royal Air Force Nursing Service[5] (PMRAFNS) 1921–50	1951–80[6]		WRAF 1918–20
Matron-in-Chief	Air Commandant		Commandant
Chief Principal Matron[7]	Group Officer		Deputy Commandant
Principal Matron	Wing Officer		Assistant Commandant I
Matron	Squadron Officer		Assistant Commandant II
Senior Sister	Flight Officer		Administrator
Sister			
Staff Nurse[8]	Flying Officer		Deputy Administrator
			Assistant Administrator

<small>NOTES</small>

1 From 1 August 1968 WRAF officers had the same rank titles as their male counterparts: the WRAF was dis-banded in 1994.
2 Introduced 1919 as Marshal of the Air, changed to Marshal of the Royal Air Force in 1925.
3 Changed to Flying Officer in 1949.
4 Changed to Pilot Officer in 1949.
5 Originally the Royal Air Force Nursing Service; became Princess Mary's in 1923.
6 From 1 April 1980, PMRAFNS officers have used the same rank titles as the RAF and WRAF, but the rank of Pilot Officer is not used.
7 In use between March 1944 and July 1948.
8 In use between January 1921 and June 1941.

Non-commissioned officers and airmen/airwomen

RNAS	RFC	WRAF, 1918–20[1]
Chief Petty Officer I	Warrant Officer	Senior Leader
Chief Petty Officer II	Quartermaster-Sergeant	Chief Section Leader
Chief Petty Officer III	Flight Sergeant	Section Leader
Petty Officer	Sergeant	
Leading Mechanic	Corporal	Sub-Leader
Air Mechanic I	Air Mechanic I	
Acting Air Mechanic I	Air Mechanic II	
Air Mechanic II	Member	

RAF, 1918	RAF, 1919–51
Sergeant Major I/Chief Master Mechanic/Chief Master Clerk	Sergeant Major Class 1[2]
Sergeant Major II/Master Mechanic/Master Clerk	Sergeant Major Class 2[2]
Flight Sergeant/Chief Mechanic/Flight Clerk	Flight Sergeant
Sergeant/Sergeant Mechanic/Sergeant Clerk	Sergeant
Corporal/Corporal Mechanic/Corporal Clerk	Corporal
———/Air Mechanic 1st Class/Clerk 1st Class	Leading Aircraftman
Private 1st Class/Air Mechanic 2nd Class/Clerk 2nd Class	Aircraftman 1st Class
Private 2nd Class/Air Mechanic 3rd Class/Clerk 3rd Class	Aircraftman 2nd Class

RAF, 1951–64[3]	RAF, 1964 to date[4]
Warrant Officer/Master Technician	Warrant Officer/Master Aircrew
Flight Sergeant/Chief Technician[5]	Flight Sergeant/Chief Technician[5]
Sergeant/Senior Technician	Sergeant
Corporal/Corporal Technician	Corporal
Senior Aircraftman/Junior Technician[6]	Senior Aircraftman/Junior Technician[6]
Leading Aircraftman	Leading Aircraftman
Aircraftman 1st Class	
Aircraftman 2nd Class	Aircraftman

PMRAFNS 1963–71[7]	PMRAFNS 1980 to date[8]	Aircrew Ranks 1946–50[9]
Chief Staff Nurse	Warrant Officer	Master Aircrew
Senior Staff Nurse	Flight Sergeant	Aircrew I
Staff Nurse 1	Sergeant	Aircrew II
Staff Nurse	Corporal	Aircrew III/Aircrew IV
Student Nurse 1	Senior Aircraftman	
Student Nurse 2	Leading Aircraftman	
Student Nurse 3	Aircraftman	

1   WAAF and WRAF ranks from 1939 on were
    similar to the male equivalents, e.g. Leading
    Aircraftwoman.

2   The rank of Sergeant Major was abolished in
    January 1933 and replaced by a single rank of
    Warrant Officer.

3, 4 NCOs and Airmen were placed into trade groups,
    and the Technician ranks were linked to trades
    involving technical skills, such as Engine Fitter
    and Musician. The traditional ranks were allo-
    cated to non-technical trades such as the RAF
    Regiment, Catering and Supply.

5   Chief Technician is a stage between Sergeant and
    Flight Sergeant.

6   Junior Technician is a stage between Senior
    Aircraftman and Corporal.

7   Before 1963 all members of the PMRAFNS were
    commissioned. In March 1971 the PMRAFNS
    ranks were changed to followed the Technician
    structure in use at that time for male nurses serv-
    ing in the RAF. In September of that year the
    Nursing trade group was split into two parallel
    schemes: those training as, or qualified as, State
    Registered Nurses followed the Technician route,
    whilst men and women qualified as or training as
    State Enrolled Nurses were allocated the tradi-
    tional RAF ranks but were unable to rise beyond
    the rank of Sergeant.

8   From 1 April 1980 all RAF nurses have followed
    the traditional rank structure.

9   The rank title used reflected the aircrew special-
    ization, e.g. Master Pilot, Navigator III, Engineer
    II, etc. Aircrew under training had the rank of
    Cadet Pilot, etc. They proved unpopular and were
    dropped in favour of the Sergeant/Flight Sergeant
    system, with the exception of Master Aircrew,
    which continues in use.

APPENDIX 2

Useful Addresses

For useful addresses relating to museums and archives associated with aviation see chapter 15.

Records of Service

ROYAL AIR FORCE

RAF Disclosures Section
Room 221b, Trenchard Hall
RAF Cranwell
Sleaford
Lincolnshire
NG34 8HB
Tel: 01400 261201, ext. 6711;
ext. 8161/8159 (officers);
ext. 8163/8168/8170 (airmen)

FLEET AIR ARM (ROYAL NAVY)

RN Disclosures Cell
Room 48, West Battery
Whale Island
Portsmouth
Hampshire
PO2 8DX
Tel: 02392 628670 or 628671

ARMY AIR CORPS

Details concerning officers and men of the Glider Pilot Regiment and Army Air Corps can be obtained from:

Army Personnel Centre
Historic Disclosures
Mailpoint 400
Kentigern House
65 Brown Street
Glasgow
G2 8EZ

Medals

Details concerning post-1939 medals awarded to members of the armed forces can be obtained from:

Ministry of Defence Medal Office
Building 250
RAF Innsworth
Gloucester
GL3 1HW

Please note that this address is due to change. For further changes use the MOD website at *www.mod.uk* for updates.

APPENDIX 3

Common Unit Abbreviations in RFC/RAF Service and Related First World War Records

The following is a list of abbreviations found in pre-1920 service records and other contemporary records relating to units of the RFC and RAF. There was no standard list of abbreviations to be used, and frequently more than one abbreviation for the same unit can be found in the same record. This lack of standardization also means that this list is far from exhaustive, but other abbreviations can often be deduced by using components of those found below. In the case of service records, the sequence of units can help (e.g. officers would be posted to a Cadet Wing or School of Aeronautics early in their service, and would often finish up at a Reserve Depot or Equipment and Personnel Depot). Details of support units of the RFC and RAF (i.e. anything except squadrons) can be found in *Royal Air Force Flying Training and Support Units* by R. Sturtivant, J. Hamlin and J.J. Halley. This volume also includes a placename index which can be useful in identifying unknown units, as placenames are frequently found in early service records.

A&IC Sch	Artillery and Infantry Co-operation School
AAC	Air Ammunition Column
AAP	Aircraft Acceptance Park
ACMB	Aviation Candidates Medical Board
ACS	Airship Construction Station or Air Construction Service
AD	Aircraft Depot
AFC	Australian Flying Corps
AG & BS	Aerial Gunnery and Bombing School
Air Min	Air Ministry
AP	Aircraft Park
ARD	Aircraft Repair Depot
Arm Sch	Armaments School
ARP	Aeroplane Repair Park
ARS	Aeroplane Repair Section
ASC	Air Service Constructional (Corps)
ASD	Aeroplane Supply Depot
BCo	Balloon Company
Bde	Brigade
BEF	British Expeditionary Force
BTW	Balloon Training Wing

BTW	Boys' Training Wing
CCH	Casualty Clearing Hospital
CD	Clothing Depot
CDD	Cadet Distribution Depot
Cdt Brig	Cadet Brigade
CFC	Canadian Forestry Company
CFS	Central Flying School
CWg	Cadet Wing
DS	Depot Squadron
ELG	Emergency Landing Ground
EPD	Equipment and Personnel Depot
ETB	Eastern Training Brigade
FIS	Flying Instructors' School
FS	Fighting School
Gp	Group
GS	General Service(s)
HD	Home Defence
Hosp	Hospital
HQ	Headquarters
HS	Home Service
KB	Kite Balloon
KBS	Kite Balloon Section
KBT	Kite Balloon Training
Med Dis	Mediterranean District
Med Off Trg Sch	Medical Officers' Training School
MT	Motor Transport
MTD	Marine Training Depot
MTDpt	Motor Transport Depot
MTRD	Motor Transport Repair Depot
NF	Night Flying
NTS	Night Training Squadron
Obs Sch	Observers' School
OCW	Officer Cadet Wing
OTTW	Officers' Technical Training Wing
Pal Bde	Palestine Brigade
RAE	Royal Aircraft Establishment
RAF	Royal Air Force
RAS	Reserve Aeroplane Squadron
RD	Reserve Depot or Recruits' Depot
Rein Pk	Reinforcement Park
Res Sqdn	Reserve Squadron
RFC	Royal Flying Corps
RLP	Reserve Lorry Park
RS	Reserve Squadron
S of A	School of (Military) Aeronautics
S of F&G	School of Fighting and Gunnery
S of TT	School of Technical Training
SA	South African
SAD	Southern Air Depot

Sch for WO	School for Wireless Operators
Sch of AF	School of Aerial Fighting
Sch of AF & G	School of Aerial Fighting and Gunnery
Sch of AG	School of Aerial Gunnery
SD	Stores Depot
SDP	Stores Distributing Park
SEA	South East Area
SMA	School of Military Aeronautics
SNBD	School of Aerial Navigation and Bomb Dropping
Sqdn	Squadron
T	Training
TD	Tent Detachment
TDS	Training Depot Station
Trg Sqdn	Training Squadron
W or Wg	Wing
W&OS	Wireless and Observers' School
WEE	Wireless Experimental Establishment
WRAF	Women's Royal Air Force

APPENDIX 4

Royal Naval Air Stations

A fuller list of Royal Naval Air Stations by placename or HMS name can be found at *http://en.wikipedia.org/ List_of_air_stations_of_the_Royal_Navy*. Information can also be found in *Shore Establishments of the Royal Navy* by Ben Warlow.

The following list of RN Air Stations lists includes those which are still in use as well as others which have closed since 1990 or which have been transferred from Admiralty to Air Ministry use and are now RAF Stations. Many names have been used more than once so it may be important to ensure the date and name are correct for the period you are researching.

HMS *Ariel*	Lee on Solent
HMS *Condor*	Arbroath (now RM Condor)
HMS *Daedalus*	Lee on Solent
HMS *Falcon*	Hal Far, Malta
HMS *Fulmar*	Lossiemouth
	(now RAF Lossiemouth)
HMS *Gannet*	Prestwick
HMS *Heron*	Yeovilton
HMS *Hornbill*	Culham
HMS *Jackdaw*	Crail
HMS *Nuthatch*	Anthorn
HMS *Osprey*	Portland
HMS *Peregrine*	Ford
HMS *Seahawk*	Culdrose
HMS *Tern*	Twatt, Orkney
HMS *Vulture*	St Merryn

You will see that many of the RN Air Stations are named after birds.

APPENDIX 5

Command and Organizations found in AIR 24

Aden
Advanced Air Striking Force
Air Training Corps
Allied Expeditionary Air Force
Allied Expeditionary Force (Air) Supreme HQ
Army Co-operation Command
Balkan Air Force
Balloon Command
Bomber Command
Burma AHQ
Ceylon AHQ
China, RAF in
Coastal Command
Desert Air Force
Egypt Command
Far East Air Force
Ferry Command
Fighter Command
Force 438
France, British Air Force
Germany, RAF
Gibraltar AHQ
Hong Kong AHQ
Iceland Command
Iraq AHQ
Italy AHQ
Levant AHQ
Maintenance Command
Malaya AHQ
Malta AHQ
Mediterranean Allied Air Forces
Middle East Air Force
Near East Air Force
Palestine and Transjordan AHQ
Signals Command
South East Asia Command
Strike Command
2nd Tactical Air Force
Tiger Force
Training Command
Transport Command
Western Desert Command

APPENDIX 6

Regimental Order of Precedence

For a comprehensive list of all regiments in order of precedence, see *British Battles and Medals* by John Hayward, Diana Birch and Richard Bishop.

Army order of precedence

The following order of precedence is applicable to the First World War period, but it also represents information that may be needed to use many of the records for the 1900–20 period. The order is based on the date specific units were originally founded. The number at the end of each infantry regiment, starting with the Royal Scots, is the original numerical identity of the unit prior to 1881 and is the number used to identify the regiment in the index of officers' Long Numbers in wo 338.

1 Life Guards
2 Life Guards
Royal Horse Guards
Household Battalion
Royal Horse Artillery
1 King's Dragoon Guards
2 Dragoon Guards (Queen's Bays)
3 (Prince of Wales's) Dragoon Guards
4 (Royal Irish) Dragoon Guards
5 (Princess Charlotte of Wales's) Dragoon Guards
6 Dragoon Guards (Carabiniers)
7 (The Princess Royal's) Dragoon Guards
1 (Royal) Dragoons
2 Dragoons (Royal Scots Greys)
3 (King's Own) Hussars
4 (The Queen's Own) Hussars
5 (Royal Irish) Lancers
6 (Inniskilling) Dragoons
7 (Queen's Own) Hussars
8 (The King's Royal Irish) Hussars
9 (Queen's Royal) Lancers
10 (The Prince of Wales's Own) Hussars
11 (Prince Albert's Own) Hussars
12 (The Prince of Wales's Royal) Lancers
13 Hussars
14 (King's) Hussars
15 (King's) Hussars
16 (The Queen's) Lancers
17 Lancers (Duke of Cambridge's Own)
18 Hussars
19 Hussars

20 Hussars
21 (Empress of India's) Lancers

The Yeomanry Regiments
Royal Artillery
Royal Field Artillery
Royal Engineers
Royal Flying Corps
Grenadier Guards
Coldstream Guards
Scots Guards
Irish Guards
Welsh Guards

Royal Scots (Lothian) 1
Queen's (Royal West Surrey) 2
Buffs (East Kent) 3
King's Own (Royal Lancaster) 4
Northumberland Fusiliers 5
Royal Warwickshire 6
Royal Fusiliers (City of London) 7
The King's (Liverpool) 8
Norfolk 9
Lincolnshire 10
Devonshire 11
Suffolk 12
Prince Albert's (Somerset Light Infantry) 13
Prince of Wales's Own (East Yorkshire) 14
East Yorkshire 15
Bedfordshire 16
Leicestershire 17
Royal Irish 18
Alexandra, Princess of Wales's (Yorkshire) 19
Lancashire Fusiliers 20
Royal Scots Fusiliers 21
Cheshire 22
Royal Welsh Fusiliers 23
South Wales Borderers 24
King's Own Scottish Borderers 25
Cameronians (Scottish Rifles) 26
Royal Inniskilling Fusiliers 27
Gloucestershire 28
Worcestershire 29
East Lancashire 30
East Surrey 31
Duke of Cornwall's Light Infantry 32
Duke of Wellington's (West Riding) 33
Border 34
Royal Sussex 35

This order of precedence is based on the *Army List* of August 1914, to which have been added a number of units created between 1914 and 1918.

A number of Irish regiments were disbanded in 1922 and other units, such as the Parachute Regiment and the Special Air Service, were created in the Second World War. In order to see more recent orders of precedence, use the *Army List*.

FURTHER READING AND WEBSITES

Books

P.E. Abbott and J.M.A. Tamplin, *British Gallantry Awards* (Dix, 1981)

A. Bevan, *Tracing Your Ancestors in The National Archives* (7th edition, TNA, 2006)

D. Birch, J. Hayward and R. Bishop, *British Battles and Medals* (Spink, 2006)

C. Bowyer, *RAF Operations 1919–1939* (William Kimber, 1988)

N. and C. Carter, *The Distinguished Flying Cross and How it was Won 1918–1995* (Savannah, 1998)

W.R. Chorley, *Bomber Command Losses Vol 1, 1939–1940* (Midland Counties Press, 1992)

W.R. Chorley, *Bomber Command Losses Vol 2, 1941* (Midland Counties Press, 2006)

W.R. Chorley, *Bomber Command Losses Vol 3, 1942* (Midland Counties Press, 2006)

W.R. Chorley, *Bomber Command Losses Vol 4, 1943* (Midland Counties Press, 2004)

W.R. Chorley, *Bomber Command Losses Vol 5, 1944* (Midland Counties Press, 1997)

W.R. Chorley, *Bomber Command Losses Vol 6, 1945* (Midland Counties Press, 2004)

W.R. Chorley, *Bomber Command Losses Vol 7, Operational Training Units, 1940–1947* (Midland Counties Press, 2002)

W.R. Chorley, *Bomber Command Losses Vol 8, Heavy Conversion and Miscellaneous Units, 1939–1947* (Midland Counties Press, 2003)

R.C. Conyers, *RAF in Action 1939–1945: Images from Air Cameras and War Artists* (PRO, 2000)

A. and P. Cormack, *British Air Forces 1914–1918* (Osprey, 2000)

B. Escott, *Women in Air Force Blue: the Story of Women in the Royal Air Force from 1918 to the Present Day* (Patrick Stephens, 1989)

W.H. Fevyer, *The Distinguished Service Cross 1901–1938* (London Stamp Exchange, 1991)

W.H. Fevyer, *The Distinguished Service Medal 1914–1920* (Hayward, 1982)

W.H. Fevyer, *The Distinguished Service Medal 1939–1946* (Hayward, 1981)

N.L.R. Franks, *Fighter Command Losses Vol 1, 1939–1941* (Midland Counties Press, 1997)

N.L.R. Franks, *Fighter Command Losses Vol 2, 1942–1943* (Midland Counties Press, 1998)

N.L.R. Franks, *Fighter Command Losses Vol 1, 1944–1945* (Midland Counties Press, 2000)

J.J. Halley, *Squadrons of the RAF and Commonwealth 1918–1988* (Air Britain, 1988)

D.V. Henderson, Major (Retd) GM, *Dragons Can Be Defeated* (Spink, 1984)

T. Henshaw, *The Sky Their Battlefield. Air Fighting and the Complete List of Allied Air Casualties from Enemy Action in the First World War* (Grub Street, 1995)

C. Hobson, *Airmen Died in the Great War 1914–1918* (Hayward, 1995)

C.G. Jefford, W/Cdr, *A Comprehensive Record of the Movement and Equipment of all RAF Squadrons and their Antecedents since 1912* (Airlife, 1988)

List of British Officers taken Prisoner in the Various Theatres of War. August 1914–November 1918 (London Stamp Exchange, reprint 1988)

M. Maton, *Honour the Air Forces* (Token, 2004)

M. Maton, *Honour the Armies* (Token, 2006)

I. McInnes and J. Webb, *Contemptible Little Flying Corps* (Naval and Military Press, 2001)

R. McNeill, *Coastal Command Losses* (Midland Counties Press, 2003)

R.C. Nesbit, *RAF in Action 1939–1945: Images from Air Cameras and War Artists* (PRO, 2000)

D. Omissi, *Air Power and Colonial Control: The Royal Air Force 1919–1939* (Manchester, 1990)

B. Pappalardo, *Tracing your Naval Ancestors* (PRO, 2002)

G. Pitchfork, *Shot Down and on The Run* (TNA, 2007)

G. Pitchfork, *Shot Down and in the Drink* (TNA, 2007)

G. Pitchfork, *Royal Air Force Day by Day* (The History Press Ltd, 2008)

W. Raleigh and H.E. Jones, *War in the Air* (HMSO, regularly updated)

N.A.M. Rodger, *Naval Records for Genealogists* (PRO, 1998)

M. Roper, *The Records of the War Office and related departments, 1660–1964* (PRO, 1998)

S. Roskill, *Documents relating to the Naval Air Service 1908–1918* (Naval Records Society, 1969)

S. Roskill, *Naval Policy between the Wars* (two vols., Collins, 1968 and 1976)

Seedies List of Fleet Air Arm Awards 1939–1969 (Ripley Registers, 1990)

Seedies Roll of Naval Awards 1939–1959 (Ripley Registers, 1999)

C. Shores and C. Williams, *Aces High* (Grub Street, 1994)

C. Shores, N. Franks and R. Guest, *Above the Trenches: A Complete Record of the Fighter Aces and Units of the British Empire Air Forces 1915–1920* (Grub Street, 1990)

C. Smith, *The History of the Glider Pilot Regiment* (Leo Cooper, 1992)

W. Spencer, *Medals: The Researcher's Guide* (TNA, 2008)

W. Spencer, *Army Records: A Guide for Family Historians* (TNA, 2008)

R. Sturtivant, *Squadrons of the Fleet Air Arm* (Air Britain, 1984)

R. Sturtivant and M. Burrow, *Fleet Air Arm Aircraft 1939–1945* (Air Britain, 1995)

R. Sturtivant and D. Cronin, *Fleet Air Arm Aircraft, Units and Ships 1920–1939* (Air Britain, 1998)

R. Sturtivant, J. Hamlin and J.J. Halley, *Royal Air Force Flying Training and Support Units* (Air Britain, 1997)

R. Sturtivant and G. Page, *Royal Naval Aircraft Serials and Units 1911–1919* (Air Britain, 1992)

I. Tavender, *The Distinguished Flying Medal: A Record of Courage 1918–1982* (Hayward, 1990)

N.G. Tucker, *In Adversity – Exploits of Gallantry and Awards to the RAF Regiment and its Associated Forces 1921–1995* (Jade Publishing, 1998)

B. Warlow, *Shore Establishments of the Royal Navy* (Maritime Books, 1992).

H. Williamson, *The Collector and Researcher's Guide to The Great War* (privately published, 2003)

R.C. Witte, *Fringes of the Fleet* (Nimrod Dix, 1997)

K.G. Wynn, *Men of the Battle of Britain* (Gliddon Books, 1989)

Periodicals

Aeroplane	Published monthly
Flypast	Published monthly
Cross and Cockade	Published quarterly

Websites

Advice about websites can be detailed or simple, but I prefer simply to flag them up as they can change and people use them in different ways.

INDEX

A

Abbott, Claude Vincent 39–40
aces 139
ADM 1 42, 74, 77, 82, 94, 101, 107
ADM 12 61, 94–5, 107
ADM 53 74
ADM 101 120–1, 125, 126, 128
ADM 104 80, 82
ADM 116 44, 74, 77, 94, 95, 101
ADM 131 61
ADM 137 61, 94
ADM 156 107
ADM 171 89, 90, 94, 103
ADM 188 43–4
ADM 196 41–2
ADM 199 74
ADM 207 74, 128
ADM 242 79
ADM 273 42
ADM 335 74
Admiralty 8
  courts martial records 107
  Surgeons' Journals 120–1, 125, 128
Afghanistan 67–8, *135, 136*
Africa 88
African General Service Medal 91
AIR 1 34, 44, 48, 51, 55, 60, 61, 64, 65, 67, 79, 80, 93, 95–6, 113
AIR 2 64, 67, 68, 80, 91, 96, 98, 100, 102, 108, 114, 116
AIR 5 64–5, 67
AIR 8 64, 67–8
AIR 10 108, 137, 138
AIR 14 115, 116
AIR 16 80
AIR 18 108
AIR 20 64, 65, 69, 70, 108, 114–15

AIR 21 108–11
AIR 24 70, 152
AIR 25 70
AIR 26 70
AIR 27 64, 68, 70, 73, 74, 77, 142, 143
AIR 28 72, 80
AIR 29 64, 67, 72, 73, 77, 125, 126, 128, 142, 143
AIR 34 69
AIR 37 69
AIR 40 69, 115, 116
AIR 41 69
AIR 43 111
AIR 44 111
AIR 49 126
AIR 50 9, 69
AIR 54 70
AIR 69 131
AIR 71 111
AIR 76 48–51
AIR 78 55
AIR 79 35, 52–5
AIR 80 9, 57
Air Battalion (RE) 15
Air Britain 144
Air Council Instructions (ACI) 108
air crashes 82
Air Defence of Great Britain (ADGB) 21
Air Efficiency Award 106
Air Force List 48, 58, 137–8
Air Force Medal 95
Air Ministry 8, 89
  courts martial records 108–11
Air Ministry Weekly Orders (AMWOs) 104
Air Observation Post (AOP) squadrons 77
air sea rescue flights 72
Air Transport Auxiliary *130, 132*
Airborne Forces Museum 131
aircrew training *142*

airmen service records
  Royal Air Force 52–5, 57–8
  Royal Flying Corps 35–6, 39–40
Airmen Died in the Great War 79
ambulance train records 125
Americans 80
area commands 21
Armoured Car Units 64
Army Air Corps (AAC) 11, 19, 23
  awards 102
  operational records 77–8
army issue LSGC 103
Army Lists 24, 32, 137
Army Printing and Stationery Service (APSS) 40
Asia 89
associations 144
atomic weapons testing 73
Australasia 89
Auxiliary Air Force (AAF) 22, 106
AVIA 5 82
awards 91–106, *142*
  gallantry and meritorious service 91–102
  long service 103–6, *142*
  prisoners of war 116–17

B

Bacon, Captain R.H.S. 15
Baillie, Paul 100
Balkans 88
Balloon Equipment Store 13
Balloon Section *see* Royal Engineers Balloon Section
Battle of Britain 98
Belgian death certificates 80

airmen service records
Bell-Davies, Squadron Commander Richard (later Vice Admiral) 94
Bismarck 74
Boer War 60, 84, 91–2
Bomber Command 21, 68
Borneo 73
Boxer Rebellion 84
Bristol fighter aircraft 21
British Empire Medal (BEM) 98
British Library 144
British War Medal 1914–20 (BWM) 85, 86
Burnt Records 35–6

C

campaign medals 83–91, *142*
casualties 79–82, 138–9
casualty clearing station records 122
Catterick Military Hospital 124
Central Interpretation Unit 69
Chastise, Operation *143*
China 60
Churchill, Winston 23
civil aviation 64
clasps 83
CN 5 128
CN 6 128
Coastal Command 21
codenames, operational 74, 77–8, *143*
colonial policing 19, 20, 64, 65
Combat Reports 9, 69, *81*
commands 21, 68, 69–70
'Losses' books 138–9
Committee of Imperial Defence 15
Commonwealth War Graves Commission (CWGC) 37, 79, 80, 132